Total project management
of construction safety, health and environment

EUROPEAN CONSTRUCTION INSTITUTE

Total project management

of construction safety, health and environment

second edition

Published by Thomas Telford Services Ltd, Thomas Telford House, 1 Heron Quay, London E14 4JD, UK, for the European Construction Institute, Sir Arnold Hall Building, Loughborough University of Technology, Loughborough, Leicester LE11 3TU, UK

First published 1992

Second edition 1995

Distributors for Thomas Telford books are
USA: American Society of Civil Engineers, Publications Sales Department, 345 East 47th Street, New York, NY 10017-2398
Japan: Maruzen Co. Ltd, Book Department, 3–10 Nihonbashi 2-chome, Chuo-ku, Tokyo 103
Australia: DA Books and Journals, 648 Whitehorse Road, Mitcham 3132, Victoria

A CIP catalogue record for this book is available from the British Library.

ISBN: 0 7277 2082 1

ECI publication TF005/2

Printed and bound in Great Britain by Galliard (Printers) Ltd, Great Yarmouth, Norfolk

FOREWORD

The Community has undergone enormous changes since 1987 when the Single European Act came into force with its legal provisions for the establishment of an Internal Market. This led to profound changes which will continue in the forthcoming period to the year 2000 which will be characterised by rapid and far-reaching changes in technologies, jobs and skills. The economy is becoming increasingly knowledge-based; manufacturing activities are being farmed out; more high added value goods are being produced (microelectronics, biotechnologies); services are taking the lion's share; and the possession and transmission of information is becoming crucial to success.

This technological revolution is associated with a new impetus towards a simplification and rationalisation of legislation at Community level.

As a result of the Single European Act, an important body of modern Community Legislation has now been enacted aimed at improving safety and health across the board, and in particular in high risk activities, such as in construction.

This up-to-date legislation includes a specific directive on safety and health at construction and building sites, and is based on he concept of preventing work accidents and occupational diseases.

It is now increasingly accepted that good conditions of safety and health is also good business. Thus the integration of safety and health measures into a total management system in the construction sector can play as important a role as for example, cost efficiency, quality assurance and environmental protection.

Dr William J Hunter OStJ FRCP FFOM MB BS LRCP MRCS
Director European Commission Directorate General V
Employment Industrial Relations and Social Affairs

oOo

The construction industry has continued to have a relatively poor health and safety performance, despite much goodwill and effort to improve it. One of the reasons for this failure has been the lack of a systematic approach to the management of risk.

In construction - as in every industry - health and safety needs to be an integral element of the business. It needs to be ingrained in a project from conception to completion, including maintenance and eventual demolition or decommissioning.

Recent European legislation - in the Temporary or Mobile Construction Sites Directive - makes this approach a legal requirement. There is now a legal duty to consider health and safety at the design stage, to have a health and safety plan from project preparation through to completion and to prepare a file which contains health and safety information for future construction work, including maintenance, extension and demolition.

This second edition of the ECI's Safety Manual has been revised to take account of this legislation. I hope readers will find that it helps them to understand how these new legal requirements underpin the good practice which this manual contains.

Stuart Nattrass
Chief Inspector of Construction, Health and Safety Executive
Chairman, HSE Construction Industry Advisory Committee

Questionnaire

Total Project Management of Construction Safety, Health and Environment
(Second Edition)

To help us assess this publication, will you please photocopy this questionnaire, complete and return it to: European Construction Institute, Sir Arnold Hall Building, Loughborough University of Technology, Loughborough, Leicestershire, LE11 3TU UK.

We may wish to contact a sample of respondents with a fuller survey.
If you do not wish to be contacted again please tick this box. ☐

Mr, Mrs, Ms, Dr, Other _____ Initials _____ Surname _____

Position _____

Organisation _____

Address _____

_____

Telephone _____ Fax _____

1   What is the size of your organisation   (Number of employees)

Less than 10	10-25	25-50	50-100	100-250	Over 250
☐	☐	☐	☐	☐	☐

2   What is the main activity of your organisation?

Client/Owner	Designer	Contractor	Other (Please Specify)
☐	☐	☐	☐ _____

3   Did you find the manual:

clear and easy to understand?		difficult to understand?
☐	☐	☐

4   Was the manual:

too detailed?	about right?	not detailed enough?
☐	☐	☐

5   Do you expect to refer to the manual:

occasionally?		regularly?
☐	☐	☐

6   Indicate any of the following statements that may apply.   This manual will:

- form part of our organisation's library of safety publications.   ☐
- be used as the basis of a number of our safety systems.   ☐
- be used in our staff training programme.   ☐
- be circulated to our staff.   ☐

7   How much of the content was relevant to the work that you do?

all	most	some	none
☐	☐	☐	☐

8   Please add any further comments on the back of the sheet

Thank you for taking the time to complete this questionnaire

CONTENTS

Introduction   1

Glossary of Terms   4

Chapter 1   Overview and the Parties Involved   10

Chapter 2   Company SHE Policy and Strategic Objectives   21

Chapter 3   Initial Concept and Project Objectives   28

Chapter 4   Design   43

Chapter 5   SHE Plan   55

Chapter 6   SHE Costs and Benefits   84

Chapter 7   Contractual Arrangements   88

Chapter 8   Assessment of Competence and Resources   99

Chapter 9   Pre-Construction and Construction Planning   116

Chapter 10   Construction   130

Chapter 11   Pre-Commissioning and Commissioning   144

Chapter 12   Handover   152

Chapter 13   Operations Maintenance and Facilities Management   157

Chapter 14   De-Commissioning, Dismantling, Demolition   169

Chapter 15   Project SHE Audit   179

Chapter 16   Project Reviews   196

Legislation   198

Bibliography and Videos   202

INTRODUCTION

ECI TASK FORCE

This guide has been produced by the European Construction Institute (ECI) to promote a genuine and sustainable improvement in the performance of the construction industry in the areas of Safety, Health and the Environment (SHE). This edition incorporates the latest European Directives and UK Legislation. It has been compiled by the European Construction Institute's Safety Health and Construction Environment Task Force. The members of the Task Force are,

J Asprey	HVCA
R T Canning	Taylor Woodrow Construction Holdings Ltd
M J Cowlin	James R Knowles
M Disney	ECIA (NECEA/OCPCA)
S Dunstan	Nuclear Electric plc
G Gaugain	Balfour Beatty Ltd
A G F Gibb (Project Director)	Loughborough University of Technology
D Hessing	ABB Lummus Crest Europe
A Meikle	John Brown E & C Ltd
C A Tjeenk Willink	Shell Internationale Petro Maatschappij B.V.
M Totterdell	Fluor Daniel Ltd
D Tubb (Chairman)	PowerGen plc
I Williams	European Construction Institute

Overall Objectives of the Document

The Task Force recognise that there is no magic formula to be applied by those seeking to improve their performance in this area. Superior SHE performance has to be earned by diligent application of well established approaches. Unfortunately for the many people injured in the industry each year it is very unusual for all the best ideas to be applied consistently on any one project or site. The aim therefore has been to compile, based on experience and best observed practice, an extensive list of the factors that should be considered, highlighting with examples the key areas that will make the most significant contribution to success.

The overall objectives of the guide can be summarised as:

- To provide a framework for the development of pro-active management of SHE in the construction industry.

- To describe a systematic approach to construction SHE management which promotes continuing improvement in SHE performance in all construction activities.

- To define the minimum SHE objectives to be considered during each construction activity.

This guide is intended for all parties involved in construction and construction related projects; from the client to individual sub-contractors involved in sections of the project. The document provides an overview of the total construction process and highlights Safety, Health and Environmental issues at each stage of this process.

The guide has been structured to reflect the main activities that form the construction process. Each chapter can be read individually or as part of the whole document. However, it is recommended that if individual sections are read on their own, that the reader reviews Chapters 1, 2 and 3 which describe the overall concepts and the relationships between the document chapters and the project stages. Chapter 5 describes the SHE Plan which is central to the control of SHE for the project. In allowing each chapter to be read on a stand alone basis it has been necessary to have some repetition within each chapter. It is hoped that this has added to the usability of the document.

The resulting document, based on best observed practice, is intended to provide guidance and suggestions from which a selection should be made that is appropriate to the project circumstances.

The words "shall" and "must" are not intended to imply that the requirement is mandatory but have been used to emphasise the recommended practice.

The guide has been written with the intention that it will be relevant to, and used on, projects throughout Europe. To that end, wherever possible, references to individual European member states legislation have been excluded from the main chapters. The section on EC Member State Legislation includes UK legislation and regulations. It is recognised that the situation in Europe is controlled through Directives issued by the European Commission, and in particular the Temporary or Mobile Construction Sites Directives.

Notwithstanding the above, it has been necessary to use the terms Planning Supervisor and Principal Contractor. These are terms from the UK legislation, the Construction (Design and Management) Regulations. The European Directive uses the term Project Supervisor to incorporate the duties of both the Planning Supervisor and the Principal Contractor for the whole project. These terms are defined in the glossary.

In reality good working practices should not be confined to any particular location. The authors consider that many of the ideas contained in this manual could be applied anywhere in the world.

Document Layout

The document layout reflects the natural progression of a construction project from inception through completion to include decommissioning and demolition. The early chapters deal with SHE issues and concepts that relate to the whole project, whilst the later chapters describe, in greater detail, more specific aspects of the construction process such as construction, commissioning, etc.

The guide has been divided into self-contained chapters that identify the key SHE issues and where appropriate describe frameworks and provide checklists for the development of SHE procedures.

The structure of the book is shown on the following diagram.

Relationship between Guide Chapters and Project Stages

Introduction

3

GLOSSARY OF TERMS

As far as is reasonably practicable

"Reasonably practicable" is a narrower term than "physically possible" and implies that a computation must be made in which the quantum of risk is placed in one scale and the sacrifice, whether in money, time or trouble, involved in the measures necessary to avert the risk is placed in the other; and that, if it be shown that there is a gross disproportion between them, the risk being insignificant in relation to the sacrifice, the person upon whom the duty is laid discharges the burden of proving that compliance was not reasonably practicable.

Audit

Formal review of systems and operations against a pre-defined checklist of headings covering all areas to be assessed and an agreed standard.

Buildability

An assessment of design details in respect of construction sequencing and activity.

Client

The person or organisation for which a construction service is being provided.

Constructability

An assessment, starting at the strategy stage of a project, of the key issues involved in building operations and works of engineering construction to enable efficient and safe management of the construction process without detriment to occupational health and the environment.

Construction

The carrying out of any building, civil engineering or engineering construction work and includes any of the following:
the construction alteration, conversion, fitting out, commissioning, renovation, repair, upkeep, redecoration or other maintenance, de-commissioning, demolition or dismantling of a structure;

the preparation for an intended structure, including site clearance, exploration, investigation (but not site survey) and excavation and laying or installing the foundations of the structure;

the assembly of prefabricated elements to form a structure or the disassembly of prefabricated elements which, immediately before such disassembly, formed a structure;

the removal of a structure or part of a structure or of any product or waste resulting from demolition or dismantling of a structure or from disassembly or prefabricated elements which, immediately before such disassembly, formed a structure; and

the installation, commissioning, maintenance, repair or removal of mechanical, electrical, gas, compressed air, hydraulic, telecommunications, computer or similar services which are normally fixed within or to a structure.

Construction (Design and Management) Regulations (UK)
These form the UK legislation implementing the EC Temporary or Mobile Construction Sites Directive.

Contract Plan
Plan detailing SHE contract strategy, such as: form of contract to be used, packaging of work elements and tender evaluation procedures.

Contractor
Contractors include subcontractors and may also be known as works, specialist, trade or nominated contractors. They have safety, health and environmental responsibilities for their own employees and others.

Corrective Action
An action that is required to correct a defect/problem in a management system/ activity.

COSHH
Control of Substances Hazardous to Health Regulations 1988 was introduced into the UK to further enhance the Safety and Health of persons who may come into contact with substances during their work activities. The scope of these regulations is wide from chemicals to petroleum, to dust, micro-organisms and carcinogens to biological agents and respiratory sensitisers.

Dangerous Occurrence
Those dangerous occurrences defined in UK regulations, Schedule 1 of the Reporting of Injuries, Diseases and Dangerous Occurrences Regulation, RIDDOR 1985, that are reportable.

Economic Screening Analysis
Financial and economic appraisal of all potential options leading to a reduction in the number of project schemes being considered.

Employment Medical Advisory Service (EMAS)	EMAS forms part of the UK HSE's Health Policy Division. It is responsible for providing advice to employers, employees and others about all aspects of health at work. It continues to give advice on all health aspects of employment and rehabilitation to the Training Agency.
Feasibility	Initial assessment of project concepts. Sensitivities of each solution to engineering, financial and SHE criteria are evaluated.
Front End	The preparation of scheme design drawings and budget costings to allow project to go out for tender.
Hand Over	Formal process of handing over the building, plant, equipment etc. to the Client. The vesting of legal ownership to the Client.
Hazard	An activity, material or process that could have adverse safety, health or environmental consequences.
Hazardous Materials	Materials which could have adverse safety, health and environmental consequences if managed, or disposed of inappropriately.
HAZCON	A formal procedure for the early identification and assessment of safety, occupational health and environmental (SHE) risk in building operations and works of engineering construction to enable all reasonable practical steps to be taken to reduce or eliminate them.
HAZOP	Hazard and operability study. A systematic technique for identifying operations and processes that have intrinsic risk.
Health and Safety Commission (HSC)	The UK Health and Safety Commission consists of representatives of both sides of industry and the local authorities. It is responsible for developing policies in the health and safety field, and for making proposals for new health and safety regulations to the appropriate minister.
Health and Safety Executive (HSE)	This is a separate body in the UK appointed by the Commission which works in accordance with directions and guidance given by the Commission. The executive also enforces legal requirements, and provides an advisory service to both sides of industry. The major inspectorates in the health and safety field are within the Executive.

Health and Safety File

(Generally referred to as the SHE File in this document)

This is a record of information for the client which focuses on health and safety. It alerts those who are responsible for the structure and equipment in it of the significant health and safety risks that will need to be dealt with during subsequent use, construction, maintenance, repair and cleaning work. This file is specifically referred to in the UK Construction (Design and Management) Regulations.

Health and Safety Plan

(Generally referred to as the SHE Plan in this document)

The health and safety plan serves two purposes. The pre-tender stage health and safety plan prepared before the tendering process brings together the health and safety information obtained from the client and designers and aids selection of the principal contractor. The health and safety plan during the construction phase details how the construction work will be managed to ensure health and safety. This Plan is specifically referred to in the UK Construction (Design and Management) Regulations.

Local Authorities (LA)

Under the Commission's guidance, local authorities enforce the legislation in allocated areas of employment. In general, these are 'non industrial activities'.

Planning Supervisor

The Planning Supervisor is a company, partnership, organisation or an individual who co-ordinates and manages the safety and health aspects of design. The Planning Supervisor also has to ensure that the pre-tender stage of the health and safety plan and the health and safety file are prepared. The Planning Supervisor is specifically referred to in the UK Construction (Design and Management) Regulations.

Principal Contractor

This is the contractor appointed by the client who has the overall responsibility for the management of site operations. The responsibility includes the overall co-ordination of site safety, health and environmental management. The Principal Contractor is specifically referred to in the UK Construction (Design and Management) Regulations.

It should be noted that the Planning Supervisor and Principal Contractor defined by the UK Regulations fulfil the functions of the Project Supervisor, Planning and Executive Phase Co-ordinators as defined in the EC Temporary or Mobile Construction Sites Directive.

FIGURE G1 Principal Parties Identified by the UK Legislation

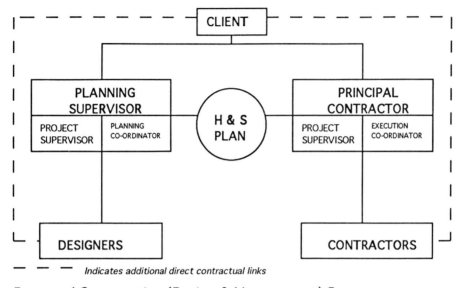

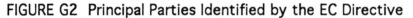

Indicates additional direct contractual links

Proposed Construction (Design & Management) Regs

FIGURE G2 Principal Parties Identified by the EC Directive

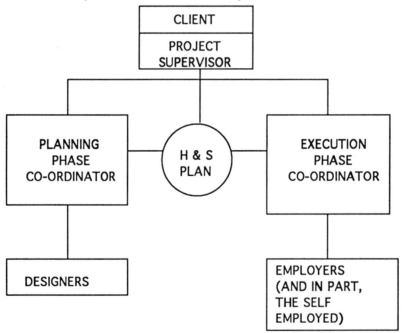

Temporary or Mobile Construction Sites Directives

Figures reproduced courtesy of the UK Health & Safety Executive, *Proposals for Construction (Design and Management) Regulations and Approved Code of Practice,* Health & Safety Commission, 10/92.

The roles are described in Figures G1 and G2.

Project
This means a project which includes or is intended to include construction work.

Risk Assessment
Identification of hazards, followed by the systematic examination of the likelihood and consequences to people, environment and assets to enable a judgement as to:

What can go wrong?

What are the concerns?

How likely is it?

Risk Control
The key factors, identified in risk assessment, that enable control of the risk, to prevent the event occurring or to contain it by mitigating against the consequences.

Appropriate engineering controls and working practices to contain the risk can then be put into place.

Risk Management Process
The options of risk avoidance by elimination or control assessed against the practicalities, costs and tolerability of the risk.

Risk includes risks to the location and safety of employees, the public and persons not in employment, but arising out of or in connection with the conduct of an undertaking.

SHE
Construction Safety, Health and the Environment.

Sub Contractor
See Contractor

Tool Box Talks
Informal meeting, between supervisor(s) and workforce, held at or near job site, to plan job tasks and discuss matters of concern to either party.

Work Permit System
A permit-to-work system aims to ensure that proper consideration is given to the risks of a particular job. The permit is a written document which authorises certain people to carry out specific work, at a certain time, and which sets out the main precautions needed to complete the job safely. It is also an essential means of communication between site management, plant supervisors and operators and those who will carry out a hazardous task.

CHAPTER 1

OVERVIEW AND THE PARTIES INVOLVED

1.1   Overview

This chapter initially presents an overview of the construction process and then defines and describes the parties involved in a typical project.

The sequence of stages in a typical construction project are:

• Concept

• Feasibility

• Front End (Scheme Design)

• SHE Plan

• Specification/Tender/Evaluation

• Execution - Construction
             - Commissioning
             - Handover
             - Maintenance
             - Decommissioning
             - Demolition

• Review

The extent to which the first three stages occur may depend on the degree of complexity of the project, but all projects will involve the subsequent stages from SHE Plan onwards. The key issues at each of these project stages are shown in Figure 1.1 together with parallel activities in engineering and project economics. It also highlights key milestones and audit points.

Table 1.1 explains and amplifies the key issues for each project stage.

The subject headings of the chapters in this guide, as applied to a typical construction project, overlap the above project stages. The position of Policy in this regard is unique in that it provides the overall corporate parameters within which the basic business processes of projects occur.

1.2   The Parties Involved

An overview of the key tasks for the individual parties is presented in Table 1.2.

The principal parties involved in construction projects are summarised as follows.

1.2.1   Clients

Client organisations may include central and local government, industrial companies, public utilities, property developers and owner/occupiers of premises.

Figure 1.1 Project Stages

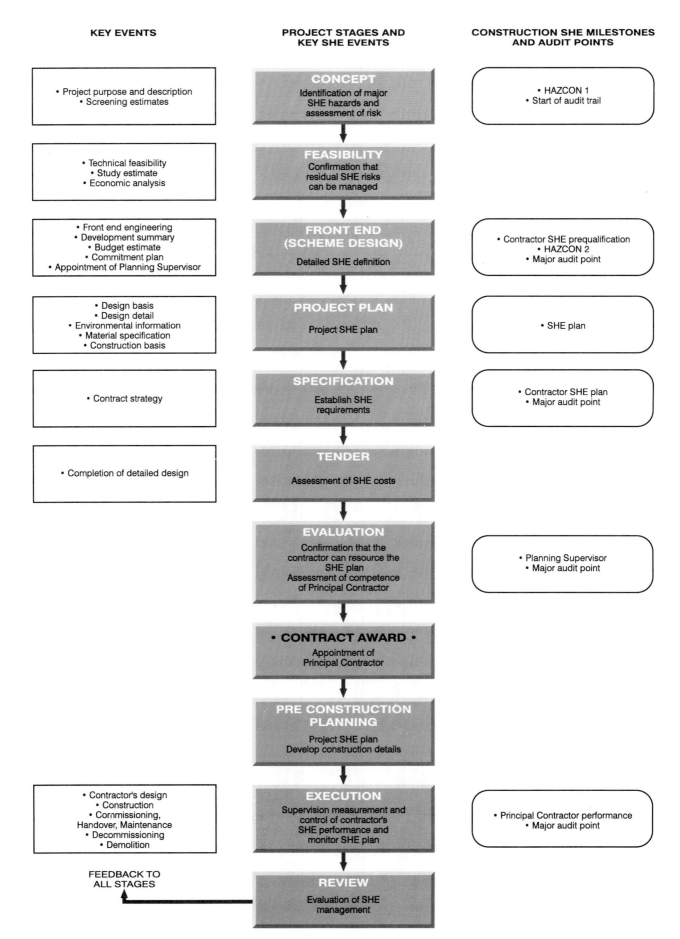

KEY EVENTS

PROJECT STAGES AND KEY SHE EVENTS

CONSTRUCTION SHE MILESTONES AND AUDIT POINTS

- Project purpose and description
- Screening estimates

CONCEPT
Identification of major SHE hazards and assessment of risk

- HAZCON 1
- Start of audit trail

- Technical feasibility
- Study estimate
- Economic analysis

FEASIBILITY
Confirmation that residual SHE risks can be managed

- Front end engineering
- Development summary
- Budget estimate
- Commitment plan
- Appointment of Planning Supervisor

FRONT END (SCHEME DESIGN)
Detailed SHE definition

- Contractor SHE prequalification
- HAZCON 2
- Major audit point

- Design basis
- Design detail
- Environmental information
- Material specification
- Construction basis

PROJECT PLAN
Project SHE plan

- SHE plan

- Contract strategy

SPECIFICATION
Establish SHE requirements

- Contractor SHE plan
- Major audit point

- Completion of detailed design

TENDER
Assessment of SHE costs

EVALUATION
Confirmation that the contractor can resource the SHE plan
Assessment of competence of Principal Contractor

- Planning Supervisor
- Major audit point

• CONTRACT AWARD •
Appointment of Principal Contractor

PRE CONSTRUCTION PLANNING
Project SHE plan
Develop construction details

- Contractor's design
- Construction
- Commissioning, Handover, Maintenance
- Decommissioning
- Demolition

EXECUTION
Supervision measurement and control of contractor's SHE performance and monitor SHE plan

- Principal Contractor performance
- Major audit point

FEEDBACK TO ALL STAGES

REVIEW
Evaluation of SHE management

TABLE 1.1 PROJECT STAGES AND KEY SHE ISSUES

Project Stage	SHE Issues	Key Questions	Key SHE Events
Concept	Identification of SHE Hazards	What SHE issues need to be considered? What SHE issues impact on the project concept?	Identification of major SHE hazards relevant to the project
Feasibility	Qualitative SHE assessment Identification of SHE issues relevant to each project option	For each project option: What could go wrong? What are the consequences of things going wrong? What is the probability of things going wrong? What are the alternatives? Can these matters be prevented? Can they be limited? Contingency plans? CAN THE SHE ISSUES BE MANAGED?	Project selected in the knowledge that the major SHE issues can be managed
Front End	Detailed SHE assessment and quantification	Can any of the identified SHE hazards be eliminated or reduced Which contractors satisfy basic SHE requirements and can be considered to carry out this project	Detailed SHE definition Contractor SHE pre-qualification
Project Plan	Project SHE issues defined and SHE management procedures developed	What SHE management systems need to be in place to manage this project effectively? What SHE performance measures should be used in auditing and measuring contractor compliance during project execution?	Detailed Project SHE Plan
Contract Plan	Contract type decision Packaging of work elements Development of SHE contract strategy	What contract strategy should be adopted to meet the project plan objectives? How is the work to be packaged and what effect does this have on SHE management? Does the chosen contract strategy effect the project plan?	Contract SHE Plan(s)
Tender	Development SHE bid evaluation criteria	What SHE factors are important to the project? How should contractor bids be assessed against SHE criteria? Which pre-qualified contractors should be invited to bid?	Specification of SHE bid evaluation criteria Bidders list of pre-qualified contractors
Evaluation	Evaluation of bidders SHE plan	Does the contractor SHE plan meet the projects requirements? Has the contractor appropriately costed the project SHE requirements? If the contractor does not currently comply, can compliance be achieved? At what cost?	Contractor selection. Agreed contractor SHE plan
Execution	Monitoring of contractor SHE performance. Review of SHE management systems	Is the contractor meeting his contractual obligations in respect of SHE? Is corrective action necessary? Are the project audit systems working? Does the SHE management system need tuning?	Supervision and measurement of contractor SHE performance. Fine tuning of contractor SHE performance
Review	Evaluation of SHE management Should be carried out throughout the project life cycle	Did the SHE plan achieve the project goals? How can the mangement of SHE be improved?	Learning. Update procedures and policy (if found lacking)

All of them may commission work in their own right and, as financiers of the construction project, have a crucial role to play in the establishment of the right conditions for the management of site work. Clients are in a position to exercise considerable control over its conduct although this may vary considerably from one of total control to one where the client relies entirely on his professional advisers, who may be nominated as Planning Supervisor and/or Principal Contractor. In each case it is crucial that the role of each person in the management team is clearly defined, including SHE responsibilities. The client has direct responsibility for ensuring the competence of such appointments and the production of a SHE Plan for the project.

Potential problems with the effective management of SHE can be prevented by client intervention either directly or through his professional advisers.

The client's key duties (as far as is reasonably practicable) are to:

- Select and appoint a competent Planning Supervisor and Principal Contractor.

- Verify the Planning Supervisor and Principal Contractor are competent and will allocate adequate resources for management of health and safety.

- Verify the designers and contractors are competent and will allocate adequate resources for management of health and safety.

- Provide the Planning Supervisor with SHE information relevant to the project.

- Ensure construction work does not start until the SHE Plan is in place and fully developed by the Principal Contractor.

- Ensure the SHE File has been collated during the project and available for handover to the client responsible for operations.

1.2.2   The Client's Agent

A person or organisation appointed by the client to act on behalf of the client in respect of the above duties.

The client's key duties (as far as is reasonably practicable) are to:

- Select and appoint a competent agent.

- Verify the agent will allocate adequate resources for SHE management.

- Provide the agent with health, safety and environmental information relevant to the project.

1.2.3   The Planning Supervisor

The Planning Supervisor may be an individual for small projects, but is likely to be an organisation for larger complex projects. The Planning Supervisor has to coordinate the SHE aspects of project design and initial production of the SHE Plan, and in particular to:

- Ensure designers comply with their responsibility to reduce risks during construction, commissioning, maintenance and demolition by identifying the hazards and detailing methods, sequences and materials to be adopted during the project.

- Ensure cooperation between designers to identify hazards at interfaces and overlapping areas of construction in order to reduce risks.

- Collate health and safety information to be incorporated into the SHE Plan.

- Provide the client with information as requested on the competence and allocation of resources by designers and all contractors.

- Ensure statutory notification of construction work to the responsible authority.

- Ensure the SHE file is prepared and available for handover to the client responsible for operation of the building, structure, plant or process.

1.2.4 Professional Advisers

These may include consulting engineers, architects, quantity surveyors, construction engineers, construction managers, occupational health and safety advisers.

One of their main tasks during construction is to ensure that the project is completed by the contractor according to plan in terms of cost, time and quality. This should include elements of SHE management and the contract terms should include allowance for the relevant SHE standards, particularly where these are identifiable and can therefore be costed.

In addition professional advisers should consider whether there are special factors such as contaminated land, temporary states of instability, etc. which could affect the health and/or safety of those doing the work and, if so, should inform the client/Planning Supervisor to include in the contract specification for prospective contractors at the tender stage.

Engineers and designers should ensure that the project is so designed that it can be built, operated, maintained and demolished safely without risk to health or environment. Particular attention should be given to providing safe access, safe places of work and safe systems of work. They should also aim to specify materials that are safer to use.

1.2.5 Designer

The designer's key duties are (as far as reasonably practicable) to:

- Comply with their responsibility to reduce risks during construction, commissioning, maintenance and demolition by identifying the hazards and detailing methods, sequences and materials to be adopted during the project.

- Cooperate with other designers to identify hazards at interfaces and overlapping areas of construction in order to reduce risks.

- Provide health and safety information to the Planning Supervisor to be incorporated into the SHE Plan.

1.2.6 Principal Contractor

The Principal Contractor could be an individual for small projects but is likely to be an organisation for larger projects.

The Principal Contractor has the responsibility for managing the health and safety during the construction stage. The Principal Contractor's key duties are to:

- Develop and implement the SHE plan for the construction site.

- Ensure competent and adequately resourced sub-contractors are appointed.

- Verify sub-contractors comply with their responsibility to reduce risks during construction, by identifying the hazards and assessing the risks detailing method statements to reduce the risks.

- Ensure cooperation between contractors to identify hazards at interfaces and overlapping areas of construction in order to reduce risks.

- Ensure statutory notification of construction work is displayed on site.

- Provide the Planning Supervisor with information for the SHE File.

- Ensure contractors comply with the site rules contained within the SHE Plan.

- Monitor the application of the SHE Plan.

- Ensure contractors are informed of the site rules contained within the SHE Plan and there is a system of regular meetings to discuss the implementation of the plan.

- Ensure only authorised persons are allowed on to the site.

1.2.7   Main Contractor/Management Contractor

A main contractor may do the work directly, or employ a number of sub-contractors, including those nominated by the client. The main contractor may have a different title in the contract such as Management Contractor.

In all circumstances, the main contractor will either be the Principal Contractor or work directly for the Principal Contractor.

The successful main contractor should examine the information supplied by the client's professional advisers and using experience and expertise, devise an economic construction method which must allow for the relevant SHE standards.

Where the work is carried out entirely by the main contractor, its staff will be responsible for the implementation of safe working methods at each stage of the work and should plan in advance for any hazardous activities.

Where sub-contractors are engaged, the main contractor has overall responsibility for the safe management of the work. Although the main contractor bears the responsibility for the coordination of the different sub-contractors' activities on site, this does not relieve sub-contractors of their own safety, health and environment responsibilities.

1.2.8   Design and Build Contractor

A design and build contractor will either be the Planning Supervisor or work directly for the Planning Supervisor. A design and build contractor may also be the Principal Contractor.

A design and build contractor will, in addition to his responsibilities for the construction of the works, have responsibilities associated with the design of the project. He will therefore take on the responsibility to ensure that the project is designed such that it can be built, operated, maintained and demolished safely, without risk to health and the environment.

The site team should continue to act as a responsible contractor, by examining the information supplied by the design team, and devising economic construction methods that fully recognise all relevant safety, health and environmental issues.

1.2.9 Contractors working for the Principal Contractor

Contractors in general have duties to cooperate with the Principal Contractor in the implementation of the SHE Plan. These duties apply whether the contractor is directly employing or using self employed persons. These duties apply to all organisations working for the Principal Contractor irrespective of the particular title used.

The key duties are to:

- Provide information for the SHE Plan about risks to health and safety arising from their work and the steps they will take to control and manage the risks.

- Manage their work so that they comply with the rules in the SHE Plan and directions from the Principal Contractor.

- Provide the Principal Contractor with information for the SHE File.

- Ensure cooperation between sub-contractors to identify hazards at interfaces and overlapping areas of construction in order to reduce risks.

- Ensure employees comply with the site rules contained within the SHE Plan.

- Monitor the application of the SHE Plan.

- Ensure employees are informed of the site rules contained within the SHE Plan and there is a system of regular meetings to discuss the implementation of the plan.

- Ensure only authorised persons are allowed on to the site.

 All contractors remain specifically and directly responsible for the safety and health of their own employees and of others who may be affected by their work.

They should not sub-contract work without the prior approval of the Principal Contractor as this would circumvent all vetting and monitoring procedures.

1.2.10 Sub-Contractor and the Self Employed

Sub-contractors may be appointed directly by the principal/main/management contractor and are often contracted to do the actual work because of their specific expertise.

The duties and responsibilities of such sub-contractors for their own employees and those under their direct control are the same as those set out for all contractors. In particular, they must cooperate not only with the contractor who appointed them but also with the Principal Contractor who has overall control of the site.

Appointed sub-contractors should not further sub-let the work to another sub-contractor without the approval of the client/Principal Contractor/main or management contractor.

Where approval is given for further sub-letting of the work, all relevant information must be distributed by the Principal Contractor so that all sub-contractors are aware of the general SHE rules and conditions laid down for the project.

TABLE 1.2 KEY ISSUES FOR THE PARTIES

RESPONSIBILITY FOR S & H OF EMPLOYEES	CLIENT	CLIENT'S AGENT	PLANNING SUPERVISOR	PROFESSIONAL ADVISORS	DESIGNERS	PRINCIPAL CONTRACTOR	MAIN CONTRACTOR	CONTRACTORS	SUB-CONTRACTORS
SHE MANAGEMENT FRAMEWORK	YES	YES	YES	YES	YES	YES	YES	YES	YES
	Select the type of contract that is best suited to the project	To act as the client	Advise client on SHE competence of designers.	Advise client on SHE performance of potential contractors	Complete design risk assessments.	Develop and implement the Health and Safety Plan.	Develop and implement the Health and Safety Plan.	Accept Principal Contractors right to manage the site.	Accept Principal Contractor's right to manage the site.
	Shortlist only Planning Supervisors and Principal Contractors that have the required SHE policy, attitude and performance.		Ensure designers complete risk assessments.	Nominate particular sub-contractors where required using agreed SHE selection criteria.	Co-operate with other designers.	Ensure contractors are competent to implement SHE Plan.	Ensure contractors are competent to implement SHE Plan.	Ensure the systems of work etc are safe and minimise risk.	Agree with Principal Contractor the SHE requirements for sub-contractors.
	Ensure that the terms of the contract include adequate financial provision to carry out the work safely to specific contract SHE requirements.		Co-ordinate designers SHE interfaces	Provide expert advice on SHE management	Co-ordinate SHE advice from professional advisors.	Ensure coordination of contractors.	Ensure coordination of contractors.	Co-operate with other contractors.	
	Provide detailed instruction to contractors at the tender stage to establish who has overall responsibility for the management of the construction work on site including any client/contractor rules/procedures to be observed.		Ensure the Health and Safety Plan is prepared.		Supply SHE information to Planning Supervisor.		Ensure details of health and safety plan are provided for contractors.	Monitor SHE performance.	
							Monitor implementation of health & safety plan.	Ensure SHE Plan is provided to employees.	
							Co-operate with Principal Contractor.		
							Produce method statements for identified hazards and risks.		

TABLE 1.2 KEY ISSUES FOR THE PARTIES

RESPONSIBILITY FOR S & H OF EMPLOYEES	CLIENT YES	CLIENTS AGENT YES	PLANNING SUPERVISOR YES	PROFESSIONAL ADVISORS YES	DESIGNERS YES	PRINCIPAL CONTRACTOR YES	MAIN CONTRACTOR YES	CONTRACTORS YES	SUB-CONTRACTORS YES
SHE MANAGEMENT FRAMEWORK (Cont'd)	Ensure the Principal Contractor has the resources to fulfil his key site SHE management role. Clearly define and allocate SHE responsibilities to each of the parties involved at each stage of the project. Ensure the appointment of an agent is verified as competent.								
DESIGN	Supply designer with identified hazards. Supply designer with project feasibility studies. Provide designer with access to all other designers across the project.	To act as the client	Ensure designers continue to co-operate. Verify the risk assessments have been completed for all activities within the project. Collate information for the health and safety plan and health and safety file.	Contribute expertise to the design team in order to produce design features which are easier to construct and are without risk to health. Identify potential construction hazards associated with design.		Continue the design risk assessment process for ongoing design work. Ensure designers co-operate across engineering disciplines.	Ensure design team has communicated any special information on SHE. Provide feedback to the design team.	Provide feedback to the Principal Contractor on design problems resulting in SHE changes.	Provide feedback to the Principal Contractor on design problems resulting in SHE changes.

TABLE 1.2 KEY ISSUES FOR THE PARTIES

RESPONSIBILITY FOR S & H OF EMPLOYEES	CLIENT YES	CLIENT'S AGENT YES	PLANNING SUPERVISOR YES	PROFESSIONAL ADVISORS YES	DESIGNERS YES	PRINCIPAL CONTRACTOR YES	MAIN CONTRACTOR YES	CONTRACTORS YES	SUB-CONTRACTORS YES
RISK MANAGEMENT	Identify major SHE hazards and provide information to the Planning Supervisor/ Designers for inclusion in specification.	To act as the client.	Ensure design risk assessments are completed and information included in health and safety plan and passed on to Principal Contractor. Highlight outstanding risks that cannot be 'designed out'.	Identify major SHE hazards and provide information for contractors in tender documents, conduct risk assessments as required. Provide specialist advice on SHE matters. Review preventive measures arising out of accident investigations.	Assess high risk activities. Identify options taken to reduce risk. Highlight outstanding issues. Ensure interface requirements are addressed in the risk assessment.	Set up site safety, health and environment organisation to assist the line management in the effective discharge of their SHE responsibilities. Manage and coordinate SHE activities to ensure that planned procedures are carried out by monitoring SHE performance. Ensure that contractors involved in high risk activities such as demolition, structural erection etc., produce effective method statements which should be assessed and monitored. Set up site wide arrangements for dealing with emergencies, safe access, lighting, control of traffic, common facilities, etc.	Identify hazards and assess the risks associated with the hazards. Plan construction methods in detail. Brief sub-contractors on SHE before starting work. Set up meeting format and schedule. Ensure adequate measures are being taken to prevent/control SHE risks. Monitor SHE performance and seek advice, where necessary, from SHE specialists.	Identify the hazards of their work and inform main/ management contractor where necessary. Provide written method statements. Assist the main/ management contractor to co-ordinate the work by liaison and consultation. Provide incident/ accident reports.	Identify the hazards of their work and inform main/ management contractor where necessary. Provide written method statements. Provide incident/ accident reports.

19

TABLE 1.2 KEY ISSUES FOR THE PARTIES

RESPONSIBILITY FOR S & H OF EMPLOYEES	CLIENT YES	CLIENT'S AGENT YES	PLANNING SUPERVISOR YES	PROFESSIONAL ADVISORS YES	DESIGNERS YES	PRINCIPAL CONTRACTOR YES	MAIN CONTRACTOR YES	CONTRACTORS YES	SUB-CONTRACTORS YES
TRAINING	Ensure client rules and procedures are incorporated in the specification health and safety plan. Provide system for supplying information on client rules and procedures to Planning Supervisor/ Principal Contractor and contractors.	To act as the client	Ensure designers are aware of major SHE issues. Ensure client objectives/ rules/ procedures are known.	Provide specialist advice on SHE training.	Review design risk assessment process and ensure competence of design team.	Ensure health and safety plan is detailed to contractor's part of the induction course.	Assess training policy and needs at planning stage. Ensure only competent and trained personnel are working on site. Provide SHE induction and training for works and sub-contractors.	Provide the necessary SHE training and monitor effectiveness.	
PLANT AND EQUIPMENT						Ensure that statutory notifications, inspections of plant and equipment are carried out at regular intervals and records kept.	Provide suitable plant and equipment to minimize SHE hazards. Ensure that statutory notifications, inspections of plant and equipment are carried out at regular intervals and records kept.		Provide evidence of statutory notification and maintenance records.
SHE COSTS AND BENEFITS	To verify that an assessment of resource, equipment and material costs have been completed.		Identify essential separately priceable SHE items eg. access scaffolding, edge protection, welfare facilities etc. Satisfy themselves that works and sub-contractors have planned and priced for carrying out work to the contract SHE requirements.	Provide specialist advice on costs and benefits of SHE.					

CHAPTER 2

COMPANY SHE POLICY AND STRATEGIC OBJECTIVES

2.1   Introduction

This chapter describes how overall company SHE policy affects the operations and decision making within an organisation. The factors that influence policy formulation are identified and a framework for the policy development described. A worked example detailing the major headings that may be included in a company SHE policy document are provided at the end of the chapter.

The company's management should define and document its SHE policies and strategic objectives and ensure that they:

- are consistent with those of any parent company (if applicable);
- are relevant to its activities, products and services, and their effects on SHE;
- are consistent with the company's other policies;
- have equal importance with the company's other policies and objectives;
- are implemented and maintained at all organisational levels;
- are publicly available;
- commit the company to meet or exceed all relevant regulatory and legislative requirements;
- apply responsible standards of its own where laws and regulations do not exist;
- commit the company to reduce the risks and hazards to health, safety and the environment of its activities, products and services to levels which are as low as reasonably practicable;
- provide for the setting of SHE objectives that commit the company to continuous efforts to improve SHE performance.

The company should establish and periodically review strategic SHE objectives. Such objectives should be consistent with the company's policy and reflect the activities, relevant SHE hazards and effects, operational and business requirements, and the views of employees, contractors, customers and companies engaged in similar activities.

The main constituents and SHE issues are shown in Table 2.1.

2.2   The Content of a SHE Policy

The activities of an operating company are more limited than those of the parent company. Therefore, its policy statement should be more focused on specific SHE issues that relate to the activities of that operating company.

The SHE policy should be clear, concise and motivating. The content should clearly express:

- what the company intends to PREVENT (using words such as: prevent, limit, protect, eliminate);
- what the company intends to IMPROVE (using words such as: create, develop, carry out, replace);
- what the company intends to COMPLY with (using words such as: comply, demand, require.

The content should distinguish between policies which are specific to the areas of Safety, Health and Environment, and those which are common to all areas. Policies which are specific to each of the areas might include:

Safety: to PREVENT all incidents that might arise through company activities.

Table 2.1   Policy Factors - Main Constituents

External Factor	Constituents	SHE Issues
Stakeholders	Employees	Organisation's duty of care
		Human resource policy and SHE
		SHE issues relating to employee selection
		Assessment of employee competence in SHE matters
		SHE induction
		SHE training
		SHE motivation and productivity
		Individual's responsibility for SHE
		Measurement of SHE performance
		Ongoing and in-service SHE training
	Shareholders	SHE contribution to return on investment
	Client/Customer	Corporate liability
		SHE policy as a reflection of management ability and capability
		SHE partnerships and relationships
	General Public	Organisation's duty of care
		Company image
		Good working practices
Business Environment	Legislation	Member State legislation
		Procurement issues/EC standards
	Competitors	Transparency of bids (SHE items)
		Fair competition
	Commercial benefits	Client/Contractor joint benefits from good SHE performance
Business Strategy	Culture	How does company culture communicate likely reaction to SHE matters?
	Organisation	Does the organisation hinder SHE policy implementation? Is it given equal weight to quality and productivity?
	Strategy	Does the organisation only react to SHE problems?
		Are the goals of the organisation compatible with SHE goals?
		Can effective SHE management provide a competitive edge?
	Management	How does management systems and structures facilitate SHE policy
	Communication	How does the management structure communicate SHE policy? Does the company learn from job to job?
	Measurement	How does the organisation measure SHE performance?
		Does SHE measurement promote good SHE management and action?
	Activities	Recognition that construction activity is riskier, in terms of SHE, than most other activities
	General Usage	How does technology affect operations in terms of SHE management?
		What are its implications on SHE policy?
		Does the company positively look for safer systems and specifications
	Training	Is specific SHE training required for new technologies?

Health: to CREATE a healthy work environment and actively promote the health and well-being of staff.

Environment: to pursue in their operations progressive REDUCTION of emissions, effluents and discharges of waste materials that are known to have a negative impact on the environment with the ultimate aim of ELIMINATING the negative impacts.

Aspects which are common to all areas include the recognition of:

- **Position of SHE in relation to other business aspects:** it is the policy of the company to conduct its activities in such a way as to take foremost account of the health and safety of their employees and of other persons, and to give proper regard to the conservation of the environment.
- **Compliance with legislation:** Companies will accept full compliance with legislative requirements as a starting point for their policies.
- **Line management responsibility:** The execution of SHE policies is a line management responsibility.
- **Assessments in planning stages:** SHE matters should be assessed before entering into new activities.
- **Client, Planning Supervisor and Principal Contractor's SHE** policies should not conflict.
- **Interests of stakeholders:** Shareholders, employees, customers and society have legitimate concerns which should be answered.
- **Regulations and industry standards:** continual improvements in the development of regulations and industry standards in SHE will come about by working with legislators and others.

In addition, a company will need to establish specific policies. These might include policies on drugs and alcohol abuse, smoking, AIDS, road safety and others. Because these policies focus on a particular SHE topic, they can be very specific in content.

2.3 The Format of a SHE Policy

A SHE policy should follow the same format as any other company policy. This means that the policy:

- should be produced in a bold, easy to read format;
- should be in the working language of staff and the work force;
- should refer to relevant company policies, standards and procedures;
- should be consistent in appearance with other company policies;
- should clearly identify the company and the business areas to which it refers;
- is usually restricted to one A4 page or A3 display of concise, action-oriented statements;
- is endorsed and dated by the senior executive of the company.

2.4 The Dissemination of a SHE Policy

The company SHE policy should be used as a basis for the formulation of departmental or functional plans and objectives.

The policy should be made easily available for company employees and external parties, as appropriate. A SHE policy should be visibly implemented within a company's management system, including SHE cases:

- all new and existing employees should receive a personal copy of the company SHE policy after an open discussion of how the contents relate to his/her function with his/her supervisor;
- the policy should be on display in/within the company premises in a prominent location.

2.5   The Life Cycle of a SHE Policy

All control systems tend to deteriorate over time or become obsolete as a result of change. This calls for the SHE policy to be regularly reviewed with emphasis on its intent, scope and adequacy. The policy should have a custodian who is responsible for this review.

2.6   Strategic Objectives

The overall strategic objectives of the management of SHE are:

- early identification of major hazards

    - The major SHE-critical areas need to be examined at an early stage in the project development so that they can be eliminated or reduced, with appropriate controls set up for those remaining hazards.

- examination of the impact of SHE in design, on construction

    - Construction hazards that can be eliminated or reduced by integrating appropriate features in design need to be identified.

- development of a SHE framework by the company for the construction and commissioning contract

    - Construction (and commissioning) hazards that are recognised but cannot be eliminated need to be made clear in construction (and commissioning) tender documents so that the magnitude and complexity of the hazards is explicitly considered in contract strategy and contractor selection.

- development of the SHE Plan by the principal contractor before site work execution

    - The framework for the SHE Plan should be included in the tender documents and subsequently used and built upon by the contractors in their bids. This should then be expanded in further detail by the successful contractor as a comprehensive plan for managing the construction (and commissioning) hazards before work is started.

- compliance with the SHE Plan during execution

    - There is a need to ensure that all areas of the SHE Plan are strictly followed. Any areas where deviations are essential must be managed effectively by use of the principles of change control.

In the commissioning phase, there are a number of additional specific objectives which reflect the transition from building a plant safely to building and operating a safe plant:

- to demonstrate the technical integrity of the facility by testing and inspection;

- to ensure that all potential hazards have been identified and assessed during the initial commissioning and that necessary controls have been put in place, resulting in a safe transition to the operating phase;

- to transfer knowledge and records from design and construction people to production and maintenance teams;

- to demonstrate that the facility operates in accordance with the intent of the design and within the design envelope.

SHE objectives should be achievable. To this end SHE aims should be consistent with other project management objectives of time, cost and quality. It may be necessary to amend the time and cost parameters of an element of work in order to achieve the SHE objectives.

The contract should be viewed as a partnership between Client, Planning Supervisor and Principal Contractor. Objectives should, wherever possible, be compatible in an attempt to avoid a confrontational situation arising. SHE management is more likely to be successful with both sides working together, in parallel.

WORKED EXAMPLE 2.1

OUTLINE POLICY STATEMENT

This worked example presents the major headings that may be included in the Company SHE policy document. This is indicative only and the principles covered in the chapter should be applied to the specific operations of the company.

Declaration of Intent

- A statement communicating Senior Management commitment to SHE and the intent to achieve strategic SHE goals.

General Policy

- General policy statement setting out the organisation's goals and attitudes to SHE issues. Identify links with QA programme where relevant.

- Summary of relevant legislation and standards. This need not be exhaustive but refer to Company's source documents which implement all relevant legislation.

- Responsibilities and duty of care to employees and others.

- Environmental issues and concerns.

Management and Supervision

- Organisation. Is a Director accountable for leading on SHE and what are the Company's arrangements for discharging SHE duties?

- Definition of overall lines of authority and responsibility. This should follow through all layers of management down to the last point of supervision, and include other competent persons' duties.

- Communication of SHE matters. This should focus on arrangements for communicating key messages to the workface and feedback from it.

- Procedures and rules. This will refer to both Company level documentation and standards and how these will be converted to site specific instructions.

- Definition of overall performance goals.

- Monitoring. The arrangements for managerial review of safety policy and performance should be described.

Training and Recruitment

- Employee selection and SHE competency assessment.

- Induction.

- Promotion and awareness of SHE matters.

- Ongoing and in service training.

- SHE professionals. Identify these at both Company and site level.

SHE Assessment and Measurement

- SHE assessment. Describe process for hazard identification and risk assessment.

- Emergency response procedures. Include environmental issues (spillages etc).

- How SHE performance will be measured. Positive measures should be included as well as incidents/accidents.

- SHE audit and inspection. Describe Company level audit, site internal/external audits, site level monitoring and self checking.

- Incident, investigation and reporting procedure.

Equipment and Methods of Work

- Specialist equipment and processes.

- Personal protective equipment.

- Systems of work (Permit Systems, etc.).

- Hygiene and housekeeping.

- New technologies.

Interfaces

- Identify key interfaces. Client, contractor, sub-contractor, employee, regulator.

- Identify arrangements for managing safety across these interfaces.

The SHE policy statement should be applicable to all operations undertaken by the organisation, for their complete life cycle, and the operations of suppliers and sub-contractors under the control of the Company.

CHAPTER 3

INITIAL CONCEPT AND PROJECT OBJECTIVES

3.1 Introduction

This chapter explains the SHE steps involved in the earliest project stages of initial concept, from a statement of project initiation to the completion of front end design and definition of the preferred option. It introduces the importance of identifying major hazards at this early stage and determining the SHE implications of the choice of project from the options available. Worked examples on HAZCON 1 and 2 procedures (a company specific systematic approach) are included at the end of this chapter.

3.2 Project Concept, Initial Risk Assessment and SHE Issues Identification

The early steps are the first formal assessment of the project and will involve, among other things, a screening review of economics and determination of project feasibility. The outline of the project concept would include such items as:
- Purpose of the project
- Site location
- Project options
- Project schedule
- Construction concepts
- Screening screening estimates
- Economic analysis

Consideration of SHE issues must also be initiated at this stage.

3.3 SHE Plan

The overall project plan will comprise:
- Design Plan
- Procurement Plan
- Construction Plan
- Commissioning Plan
- Maintainability Plan
- De-commissioning Plan
- Demolition Plan

For examples of SHE Plans see Chapter 4

It is recommended that some Construction input form part of the design team to add the necessary expertise.

At this stage the proposals for managing the critical areas of SHE should also be defined, including policy and organisation. For example:

Policy	Draw the statement of project briefs on SHE that are to be observed.
Organisation	Define the formal structure for planning, communication and responsibilities for SHE, particularly between the Client and the Contractor.
Safety	Define the basis on which the occupational health programme will be developed.
Environment	Develop an environmental impact profile and establish the basis for preparation of further studies.

Figure 3.1 is a flowchart of the sequence of SHE activities in the conceptual and planning stages of a construction project together with the parallel engineering and economic activities.
The SHE File will be initiated at this stage and notification of the project to the relevant authority should be made by the Planning Supervisor.
An initial risk assessment must be made, which will be preliminary and based on limited information. The structured sequence for the evaluation of these risks is defined by the hazard identification, risk assessment and control activities described below (Hazard Identification and Risk Management Process). This sequence forms a common theme throughout the project and the material generated under these headings will become progressively more detailed as the project progresses.

3.3.1   Risk Control

Eliminate or control the risks (Is there a better way ? How to prevent It ?)

3.3.2   Incident Recovery

Establish methods for recovery in the event of loss of control (How to limit consequences ? How to recover ?).
At this stage, risk management is largely devoted to the identification of major hazards that could arise in the consideration of various project options, experience gained from previous projects should be used as an aid to this assessment by reference to:

- Close out reports from similar projects

- Similar activities in nearby or other relevant countries

- SHE audits carried out in recent years on relevant activities

- Accident statistics

- General background information on the planned areas of operations

- Published guidance by enforcing authorities.

Figure 3.1 Project Stages

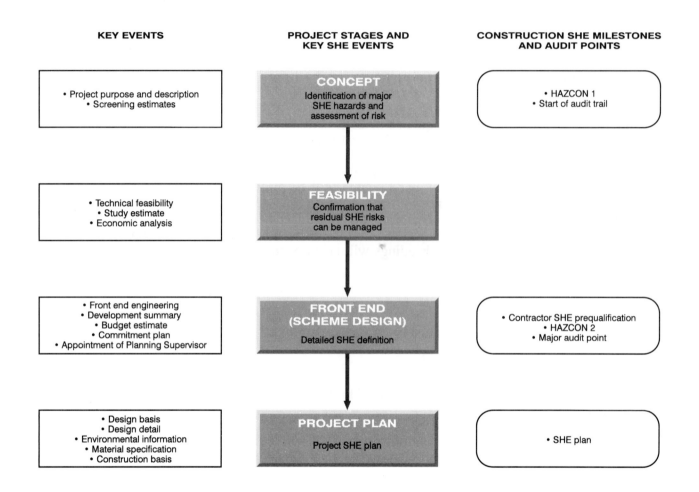

KEY EVENTS	PROJECT STAGES AND KEY SHE EVENTS	CONSTRUCTION SHE MILESTONES AND AUDIT POINTS
• Project purpose and description • Screening estimates	**CONCEPT** Identification of major SHE hazards and assessment of risk	• HAZCON 1 • Start of audit trail
• Technical feasibility • Study estimate • Economic analysis	**FEASIBILITY** Confirmation that residual SHE risks can be managed	
• Front end engineering • Development summary • Budget estimate • Commitment plan • Appointment of Planning Supervisor	**FRONT END (SCHEME DESIGN)** Detailed SHE definition	• Contractor SHE prequalification • HAZCON 2 • Major audit point
• Design basis • Design detail • Environmental information • Material specification • Construction basis	**PROJECT PLAN** Project SHE plan	• SHE plan

After the potential hazards have been established the broad SHE issues can be identified. It is useful to do this with reference to a checklist of headings to ensure thorough and comprehensive coverage.

An example summary list of headings for such a checklist is shown below.

Safety	Health	Environment
Climate	Infections	Emission
Natural Hazards	Hygiene	Effluents
Transport	Housing	Wastes
Security factors	Medical facilities	Noise and Vibration
Unskilled labour	Potable water	Light
Major risk factors	Chemicals	Damage to
e.g heavy lifts		surroundings
Excavations		Contaminated ground
Demolition		Heat
Concurrent operations		Electricity
Lifting and handling		Pressurised Systems
Confined sites		

Implementation of this checking process should highlight those areas of SHE that require particularly close attention and that should therefore be incorporated into the subsequent SHE.

3.3.3   Hazard Identification

Identify the possible hazards associated with an activity (What could go wrong ?).

3.3.4   Risk Assessment

Analyse the hazards to assess their frequency of occurrence and significance of consequences (How serious will it be ? How probable is it ?).

3.4   SHE Plan Check List

The output from Chapter 3 is the SHE input to the overall project plan. The SHE plan should be divided into main components for which the following are guideline headings:

3.4.1   SHE Management and Leadership

•   Organisation

•   Communications

- Meeting programme

3.4.2 SHE Organisation and Rules

- Policy Statement

- Legislation

- Standards

- Procedures

- Basic rules
- Health, Medical and Welfare Program

- Auditing

- Environmental

- Sub-contractors and Contractors

3.4.3 SHE Risk Assessment and Management

- Hazard Identification

- Risk Assessment

- SHE Performance and Measurement

- Emergency response procedure

3.4.4 SHE Training

- Employee Orientation Programme

- Promotion and Awareness

- Training Program

- Involvement of Professionals

3.4.5 Personal Protective Equipment

- Risk Assessment, PPE Requirements and PPE Use

3.4.6 Incident/Accident/Injuries Records and Data

- Incident Reporting Procedure

3.4.7 Equipment Control and Maintenance

- SHE Equipment and Equipment SHE Inspection

- Hygiene and Housekeeping

WORKED EXAMPLE 3.1

HAZCON DEFINITION AND CHECKLIST

Definition of HAZCON

A formal procedure developed by one company for early identification and assessment of safety, occupational health and environmental (SHE) hazards in building operations and works of engineering construction to enable all reasonably practical steps to be taken to reduce or eliminate the risk.

HAZCON 1

HAZCON 1 is carried out to identify major hazards to client personnel, contractors, visitors, or general public - (applying inside or outside the site boundary) together with actions/recommendations for hazard elimination or reduction. It uses checklists as an aide memoire and is carried out as early as possible in the project but in any case before the project scope and site are fixed.

HAZCON 2

HAZCON 2 is carried out to provide a detailed assessment of construction hazards based on the completion of a significant level of engineering definition but at least including plans and elevation together with draft overall construction method statement, contract plan, project programme and site layout drawings. It should also include a review of HAZCON 1 results to see whether the development of the scope of the project has added or removed any major construction hazards.

HAZCON 1 CHECKLIST

Project Title				
Project Number		Date	Tick if applicable	
Factors to be considered during Construction			Within the works	Outside the works
ENVIRONMENT				
Contaminated Ground				
Unstable Ground				
Existing Underground Services				
Access Routes - Vehicles, Personnel, Emergency				
Climatic Conditions - Cold, Heat, Rain, Lightning, Darkness				
Cultural Factors				
Waste Disposal				
IDENTIFY MAJOR RISK FACTORS				
Work At Height				
Work Over Water				
Work in Confined Spaces				
Very Large Lifting Operations				
IDENTIFY MAJOR RISK SUBSTANCES				
Lead				
Asbestos				
Radiochemicals				
PCB's				
Flammables				
Other				
RISKS TO EXISTING FACILITIES ARISING FROM CONSTRUCTION WORK				
Noises/Disturbance				
Vibration				
Emissions				
Fire				
RISKS TO CONSTRUCTION WORK ARISING FROM EXISTING FACILITIES				
Explosion				
Fire				
Emissions				
Electromagnetic Radiation				
Chemical Contamination				
Biological Risks				
RISKS AT COSTRUCTION/COMMISSIONING INTERFACE				
Testing				
Phased Handover				
Fumigation				
Author:				

HAZCON 2 CHECKLIST

A. SUMMARY OF TOPICS

1. Review HAZCON 1 report.

2. Review "site establishment safety planner" (Company in-house planning check).

3. Review draft overall method statement.

4. Review project programme.

5. Review selected drawings (plan and elevations).

6. Review Draft Contract Plan and safety requirements to be included in site contracts.

7. Discuss effects of site constraints.

8. Discuss options for minimising scope of site work.

9. Discuss testing, pre-commissioning, commissioning and eventual demolition.

10. a) Write-up recommendation for alterations to:

    - overall method statement
    - contract plan
    - programme
    - design
    - scope of site work

    b) Assess remaining risks and document actions required to reduce them.

11. Confirm method for the following up of recommendations.

B. TYPICAL RECOMMENDATIONS FOR ACTION

1. Design to be reconsidered or reviewed.

2. Restriction to be placed on allowable construction/demolition techniques.

3. Modify design programme to simplify access requirements or otherwise improve sequence.

4. Modify construction programme to reduce congestion/numbers exposed to risk.

5. Requirements for detailed method statement to be prepared before work begins to be included in the relevant contract.

6. Contractor to assess personal protective equipment (PPE) requirements and supply details to construction management. Use of PPE to be closely monitored on site.

7. Activity to be closely monitored on site.

Continued/....

C. OVERALL CONSTRUCTION METHOD STATEMENT

A broad description of how the construction/demolition will be done, taking into consideration:

- **Sequence**
  - Time
  - Work Packages
  - Orientation of Work Flow
  - Split into Areas/Floors

- **Access**
  - People
  - Plant and Equipment
  - Material
  - Maintenance of Clear Routes
  - Hydraulic Platform
  - Scaffolding/Edge Protection
  - Stairs (Early Installation)

- **Storage**
  - Off-loading
  - Set Down and Material Storage Areas
  - Security
  - Control of Materials

- **On-site Fabrication**
  - Workshop Facilities
  - Weather Protection

- **Feed Points**
  - Openings
  - Logistics
  - Site Roads (Early Installation)

- **Lifting & Transport**
  - Cranes (Mobile or Fixed) and multi-crane operations
  - Hoists (Personnel/Material)
  - Fork Lift Trucks, Excavators, Lorries

- **Shared Scaffolding**
  - Requirements
  - Contractual Implications (Responsibility Client or Contractor)
  - Safety Implications

- **Lighting**
  - External
  - Internal (Natural Light)
  - Working During Hours of Darkness
  - Congestion
  - Early Installation

Continued/....

HAZCON 2 CHECKLIST (Continued)

- **Multi-Service Gang**
  - Cleaning
  - Maintenance of Safety Equipment

- **Working Hours/Shiftwork Arrangements**
  - Supervision
  - Emergency Facilities
  - Safety/Productivity rates

- **Construction Management Arrangements**
  - Contract
  - Manning
  - Qualifications

- **Shared Welfare Facilities**
  - Medical
  - Compound
  - Offices
  - Fire
  - Canteen
  - Toilets
  - Washing Facilities

- **Temporary Power**
  - Electric
  - Pneumatic

- **Waste Disposal**
  - Asbestos/Contaminated Waste
  - Dirt Chutes/Skips

- **Fire and Emergency Precautions**
  - Fire Tender/Ambulance Access (to Works and Construction Site)
  - Alternative Escape Routes
  - Labelling/Signs
  - Detection/Alarms (Early Installation)
  - Fire Extinguisher
  - Toxic Gas Escapes (Refuges and Communications)
  - Minimising Stored Flammable Materials

- **Demarcation**
  - Barriers
  - Signs

- **Commissioning and Handover**
  - Establish Responsibilities of Contractor/Client
  - Phased Start-Up
  - Powering Up

Continued/....

HAZCON 2 CHECKLIST (Continued)

- **Control of Work**
  - Permit to Work Arrangements

D. HAZCON 2 PROGRAMME EXAMINATION

- **Design Requirements**
  - Feedback areas of design required earlier for construction safety reasons

- **Construction Overlaps**
  - Guide Words
    - in the same area
    - above
    - at the same time
    - early
    - late
    - incorrect

E. HAZCON 2 CONTRACTS

- **Specification for Safety**

- **Site Rules and Procedures**
  - Confirm which rules and procedures apply
  - What replaces Client Procedures that will not be used?
    (e.g. Management Contracting)
  - Basis for not requiring procedures

- **Contract Package Philosophy**
  - Number/Size of packages
  - Shared facilities

- **Individual Work Place Package Requirements**
  - Supervision
  - Interfaces
  - Programme overlaps

- **Prequalification**
  - Safety Policy
  - Safety Record

- **Method Statement, Control of Substances Hazardous to Health Assessments**

Continued/....

HAZCON 2 CHECKLIST (Continued)

F.   EFFECT OF SITE CONSTRAINTS

Consider the:-

Effect of:	**On:**
Water	Enabling Works
Existing Buildings	Additional Money
Boundaries	Additional Time
Cliffs	Programme
Roads	Overall Method Statement
Railways	Location/Access
Contaminated Ground	Layout & Boundary
Unstable Ground	Design Details
Climatic Conditions	Offsite Fabrication Philosophy
Overhead Services	Storage
Underground Services	

People
- Client
- General Public

Operating Plants

Ecology

Public Utilities
- Gas
- Water Drainage
- Telephone
- Electricity

G.   MINIMISE SCOPE OF SITE WORK

- **Off Site Fabrication**
  - Vessel Dressing
  - Packaged Equipment
  - Pre-Assembled Units
  - Toilet Units
  - Audit of Fabricators Safety Systems
  - Pipework/Bridges
  - Control Rooms
  - Lagging

Continued/....

HAZCON 2 CHECKLIST (Continued)

- **Design Out Labour Intensive Work**
  - Prefinished Partitions
  - Prepainted Items

- **Build in Access**
  - Pipe Bridges Including Walkways
  - Staircases (Early)
  - Platforms
  - Steelwork - Manlock Fixings
  - Edge Protection

- **Mechanisation**
  - Hoists
  - Equipment/Plant
  - Automatic Welding
  - Hydraulic Platforms

H. TESTING

- **Pressure Testing**
  - Temporary Welds
  - Pneumatic Testing
  - Water Leaks

- **Control Electrical Testing**
  - Permits
  - Safe System

- **Load Testing**
  - Lifts
  - Cranes, Runway Beams

I. PRE-COMMISSIONING

- **Cleaning Operations**
  - Control of Substances Hazardous to Health
  - Acid Cleaning
  - Steam
  - Blowing (Noise)
  - High Pressure Jetting
  - Pigging
  - Permits

- **Light Running of Conveyors**
  - Guarding (Regulatory Requirements)
  - Trip Systems

Continued/....

HAZCON 2 CHECKLIST (Continued)

J.   COMMISSIONING

- **Introduction of Cleaning and Process Materials**
  - Control of Substances Hazardous to Health
  - Chemical Reactions
  - Emergency Shutdown
  - Dealing with Spillage
  - Flammables
  - Fumigation

K.   DEMOLITION

- Consider decontamination and structural aspects of the eventual demolition of the plant/buildings.

HAZCON 2 CHECKLIST (Continued)

CHAPTER 4

DESIGN

4.1   Introduction

This chapter develops a systematic method to identify construction, operation, maintenance and demolition hazards. Designers can then quantify the risk and develop a framework within which design, specification and planning of project and operation activities can either be used to prevent such hazards materialising or be employed to mitigate their effects.

Recommendations arising from such risk assessments should be available in the early phases of design when site layouts, detailed design drawings, schematics, specification criteria, etc., are still being developed.

These assessments must include identification of design errors, ambiguities and/or omissions. Questions of ambiguity and omission are especially important since the definition of design work and its separation from the construction phase is not always clear. In some disciplines, for example structural engineering, parts of the design are not fully detailed by the designer but are subsequently completed or amplified during fabrication and/or construction. However, it is still essential that the intent of the designer is clear and confirmed by any subsequent detailing work and that it is consistent with the proposed construction method.

It is envisaged that designers may have to obtain advice from professional advisors in order to complete the design risk assessments. As experience in the risk assessment process is developed by designers then more comprehensive criteria can be produced and a greater reduction in problems at the construction stage. Unsafe site practices can often be traced to lack of communication of the design intent from designer to detailer or a failure by the designer to examine the buildability of his design.

A worked example, examining the application of risk assessment of the design for a structure or process plant is included at the end of the chapter.

A worked example using a descriptive approach to examine the application of design to the safe erection of steel structures is included at the end of the chapter.

4.2   Design - Hazard and Effect Management Process

4.2.1   Hazard Management Process

This is defined as identification of the hazard, then assess the risk taking measures to reduce the risk and finally management controls to contain the residual risks.

4.2.2   Hazard Identification

To assemble the hazards in a tabular form, identify the activities associated with planning construction, operation, maintenance and demolition activities and show the connection with risk assessment. Hazards information can be derived from :
* Review of previous costs of hazard/risk problems, incident reports including near misses, accident reports .
* Use of existing standards and codes of practice.
* Reliance on experience: Reviews with Project professionals, for example: Architects, Civil Structural Engineers, Mechanical (piping, structural, process), C&I, Chemical/Process, Fire specialists and safety engineers.
* Generic checklists;e.g.
(HAZCON 1 & 2 -see chapter 3)
(HAZOP Studies -see chapter 11)

Generic hazard categories listed below can be broken down into further detail as required for each type of specific plant / structure construction work.

Hazard Categorisation

Physical (P):	Hydrocarbons Under Pressure
	High Pressure Liquids or Gas
	Operations in Water
	High temperature or Cryogenic Fluids
	Hazardous Surfaces
	Ignition Sources
Chemical(C):	Explosive
	Explosive Gas Generators
	Ignition Sources
Electrical(E):	Ignition Sources
	Hazardous Equipment
	Electrical energy
Biological(B):	Toxic Substances
	Biological Hazards
	Asphyxiating Atmospheres
Environmental(EN):	Ground Conditions
Ergonomic(ERG):	Elevated Objects
	Working at Height
	Hazardous Surfaces
Mechanical(M):	Transport
	Hazardous Equipment
	Elevated Objects
Security(S):	Public Access

4.2.3   Risk Management Process

The risk management process is a systematic method for assessing the hazards that could arise during construction. Here it is used to determine the construction SHE requirements that require incorporation in the design and specification. The method should also identify those elements where SHE hazards cannot be designed-out and which must therefore be controlled by other management systems such as work procedures.

The process comprises the following steps.

- Identify the SHE critical construction activities and break down the work processes into component stages.
- Identify the hazards in these component stages that could lead to accidents based on previous annual statistics for the construction company, industry and associated work. Also the use of generic hazards and industry guidance on risks.
- Eliminate or control the hazards by the development of protective measures in the design and specification of safer materials.
- Provide special precautionary measures for those aspects that cannot be eliminated by design development.
- Define contingency plans for the precautionary measures.

Where practicable, Principal Contractor input should be sought at this stage.

The results of the Hazard Identification & Risk Management Process will be reflected in:

- Detailed design drawings and documents.
- Communication of design intent, particularly where design detailing is passed to the contractor such as in structural steelwork.
- Identification of key interfaces between client, Planning Supervisor, Principal Contractor, contractors and sub-contractors.

The assessment of risk associated with identified hazards is:
A qualitative estimate usually in the form of a matrix showing probability against consequence.

Once the identification of a high risk category has been identified for a particular activity then it is for the designer to supply the information on how the risk can be eliminated, reduced by the design. If the risk cannot be eliminated or reduced by design then a construction management procedure may be required to be developed by the Principal Contractor to control the risk.

The safest option for controlling the identified risks can be decided by the Planning Supervisor. The Planning Supervisor has to co-ordinate the health and safety aspects of **design and planning.**

In the course of the above analysis the designer may provide a number of options which have to be reviewed by the Planning Supervisor with respect to project SHE objectives. As the decision may affect the overall technical objectives of the project then the client will have to agree to the level of residual risk. The scope for pre-assembly or modules is an important consideration to reduce the site risks.

This process will be required for:
•   The design of the method of constructing the material input components.
•   The design for commissioning /handover of the process /plant
•   The design of the method for maintaining and managing the facility
•   The design for decommissioning and demolition of the material input systems.

A quantitative analysis which requires the systematic development of numerical estimates of expected consequence and probability of risk. This usually requires specialised computer software and expertise.

4.2.4   Measures to Reduce Risk

Once the risk has been prioritised for reduction then the options for the designer are:
•   Removal.
•   Replacement with a lower category risk.
•   Highlight the residual risk.
•   Identify a risk procedural method.

(All the solutions will be within the defined objectives in the SHE Plan. The options chosen will be subject to a cost/benefit analysis).

The designer should ensure the SHE Plan for the Project is adjusted to reduce risks caused by sequential activities, identify activities which will require additional controls e.g. method statements and techniques which will require specific training for operatives.

4.3   SHE Management of Design - A Framework

This section describes a framework that will allow the incorporation of construction SHE into the design. However, to ensure successful application the following approach must be taken.

•   The design team must be aware of and understand the SHE goals and policies of the Client.

•   The client or contractor must, advised by the Planning Supervisor/Project Manager, must confirm the capability of the designer ,where the former has responsibility for the design . The appointment of a designer must be subject to validation checks of capability to address SHE issues e.g. qualifications, experience, resources and knowledge of current health safety and environmental legislation.

•   During scheme design the SHE critical construction activities must be identified.

- Each identified activity should be systematically assessed using techniques such as Hazard Management Process.

- Constructability assessments should be carried out, including where available, a review of method statements to identify SHE hazards.

- The overall SHE plan for the project must be used by the designer to provide the necessary information for the next phase of the project. This way the designer can highlight areas where the risk can only be reduced by management controls, specific training or detailed method statements.

4.3.1   Designers Management Controls

Sequencing relationship between design and construction

- Contract strategy
  - Management contracting
  - Design and build
  - Conventional contracting

Allocate resources
Ensure the SHE training requirements are satisfied.
Detail the method of work for high risk activities
Coordinate the interface design requirements and define responsibilities.
Specify the designer requirements for control of commissioning

4.4   Framework

4.4.1   Hazard Identification

The major construction SHE issues which interface with design are:

4.4.2   Initial Planning

- Proximity to other activities
  e.g. Motorway construction
      Work adjacent to railway track
- Proximity to other buildings
- Proximity to plant and equipment
- Proximity to overhead or buried services
- Access restrictions
- Work space restrictions
- Geotechnical factors relating to construction activities

4.4.3   Technical Design

- Stability
- Redundancy
- Detailing
  - Interfaces and connections
  - Components
      e.g. Steel haunch details
- Errors and omissions
- Specification of safer materials e.g. non-fragile roofing materials, water-based paints

4.4.4   Constructability

- Tolerances
- Sequencing of activities
  - Due to design considerations
- Cost / Value engineering
- Work place access
  - Maximum component sizes
- Work place rules
- Statutory and regulatory requirements
- Contract packages
  - Design of interfaces between work packages
- Choice of materials

4.4.5   Construction Methodology

- Scheme management
- Comprehensive definition of responsibilities and authority
- Detailed method statements
  - Design of temporary works
  - Erection sequences
- Stability
- Materials handling
- Defence against unsafe acts
- Provision of suitable plant and equipment including PPE
- Contingency planning

4.4.6   SHE Critical Construction Activities

Examples of construction activities that have high safety and health risk associated with the work and therefore need particularly close attention by the design team are:

- Steel Erection
  - Instability of partially erected structures
  - Falls from structures
  - Falling materials and dropped objects
  - Erection sequence
- Scaffolding
- Temporary works
- Falsework and formwork
- Health Hazards
- Concurrent Operations
- Working at height
  - Roof edge falls
  - Falls through fragile roof materials
  - Falls from internal roof structures
  - Work in adverse weather
- Demolition
- Excavations and groundworks
  - Underground hazards
  - Adjacent buildings
  - Flooding
  - Side protection
  - Unidentified objects
  - Access and escape
- Tunnelling

In order to ensure that all construction sequential activities have been addressed a detailed breakdown is required from the designer, suppliers and constructors.

4.4.7   Risk reduction

The designer may be required to detail the safe system of work in the form of a method statement after completing the hazard identification/ risk assessment process.

- Method statements will address items such as:
    - Stability
    - Erection
    - Protection from falls
    - Stacking and storage of materials
    - Scheme management
    - Means of access and egress
    - Safe place of work
    - Type of plant to be used
    - Control of hazardous substances.

WORKED EXAMPLE 4.1

SHE DESIGN RISK ASSESSMENT

An outline for Design Risk Assessment is described below. This procedure has been simplified and adapted from the Project Design Risk Assessment Manual, also available from the European Construction Institute. This example is indicative only and reference should be made to the full Risk Assessment Manual.

STEP 1

The 'Hazard Activity Checklists' are targeted at specific design disciplines. Use the index numbering system to locate the sub-area/sub-group areas to be addressed by your design discipline within the manual.

STEP 2

Having identified (from Step 1) the sub-areas/sub-groups to be addressed by your particular design discipline, please find the first of these, and turn to the 'Areas of Concern' page (the first page subsequent to the title sheet within the sub-area/sub-group).

This step is diagrammatically illustrated on Figure 4.1.

Substep 2.1   (Refer to Figure 4.1)

The upper half of the 'Areas of Concern' section (titled 'Problems/Considerations') describes particular potential problems associated with the sub-area/sub-group. Please read these in order to become familiar with the potential problems. Please note that the potential problems are indicative and consequently are by no means exhaustive, and therefore you need to consider other potential problems which could arise in your particular project.

Substep 2.2

Now refer to the 'Hazard/Activity Checklist' (on the right of Figure 4.1). This checklist shows the activities and/or plant items and potential hazards associated with the sub-area/sub-group. The most significant cells of the checklist are highlighted by a bold border.

Each highlighted cell has associated with it one ore more possible design solutions, which would help to remove or mitigate the potential hazards identified. These can be found on the 'Option Suggestions' section on Figure 4.1. Please note that the solutions described are by no means exhaustive, and you should consider your own possible solutions to remove or mitigate hazards.

Remember to review all activities and/or plant items on the 'Hazard/Activity Checklist', and decide whether any cells in addition to those highlighted could be important for your particular project. Draw a border around (i.e. highlight) all cells you consider to be important for your project.

A qualitative risk assessment for all highlighted cells now needs to be carried out, as described in substep 2.3 below.

Substep 2.3

The activities/hazards referred to within the highlighted cells must be qualitatively assessed for the potential risk to the health and safety of personnel and to the environment. This requires your consideration of the **likelihood** and the **severity of potential consequences** of the hazard.

Assessment of the risk is made by using the risk assessment key below (which is also located below each Hazard/Activity Checklist in the manual).

Risk Assessment Key

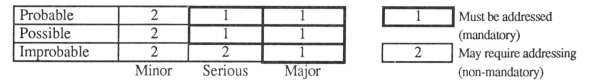

Probable	2	1	1		1	Must be addressed
Possible	2	1	1			(mandatory)
Improbable	2	2	1		2	May require addressing
	Minor	Serious	Major			(non-mandatory)

Hazard likelihood should be qualitatively judged as follows:

Probable   Will occur several times

Possible   Could occur sometimes

Improbable   Very unlikely to occur

Hazard Consequence Severity should be qualitatively judged as follows:

Minor   Slight or minor injury either to employees or to the public, e.g. bruising, cuts. No lost time accident.
Minor environmental impact, e.g. temporary excursion from target discharge levels.

Serious   Moderate injury either to employees or to the public with full recovery, e.g. a lost time accident.

Major   Loss of life potential or severe injury either to employees or to the public with long term damage.
Severe pollution. Significant clean up, disposal monitoring, assessment and liability costs.

For example, if you judge the likelihood of a potential hazard to be 'possible', and its consequence severity to be serious, from the Risk Assessment Key above, it can be seen that this would be risk rated as '1'.

Indicate the estimate risk (by inserting a '1' or a '2' in the highlighted cells) on the checklist until all the highlighted cells are complete, as shown on example in Figure 4.2.

The risk assessment is now complete, and the Hazard/Activity Checklist must be signed and dated at the bottom of the page - *Signature 1*.

Substep 2.1

A table highlighting areas of concern ('Problems/ Considerations'), which describes the possible problems associated with the sub-area/sub-group.

Substep 2.2

A table which presents possible solutions ('Option Suggestions') for those cells which have been highlighted in the Hazard/Activity.

2.1 and 2.2 above constitute the 'Areas of Concern' page.

Source: Powergen Plc 1994

Substep 2.2

A checklist of activities/ plant items and potential hazards (the Hazard/ Activity Checklist) on which the most significant cells have been highlighted

Substep 2.3

Risk Assessment Key, used to carry out a qualitative risk assessment on those activities which could result in potential hazards to personnel and the environment.

Risk grade is deliberately kept simple

COMMISSIONING, OPERATIONS AND MAINTENANCE
SUB-AREA/SUB-GROUP: ELECTRICAL AND POWER

ELECTRICAL AND POWER ELECTRICAL

PROJECT TITLE:
AREA/GROUP:
SUB-AREA/SUB-GROUP:
DESIGN DISCIPLINE:

Drawing Ref No:
Drawing Revision No:

Figure 4.1 – Illustration of Step 2

51

COMMISSIONING, OPERATIONS AND MAINTENANCE

PROJECT TITLE:
AREA/GROUP:
SUB-AREA/SUB-GROUP: ELECTRICAL AND POWER
DESIGN DISCIPLINE: ELECTRICAL

Drawing Ref No: ....
Drawing Revision No: ....

	CHECKLIST	ACTIVITY/PLANT	TRENCHES/DUCTING	CABLES	GENERATORS	TRANSFORMERS	SWITCHGEAR	HV APPARATUS	BATTERIES	SUBSTATIONS	ELECTRO. PRECIP.	INTERFACES			
	HAZARD		a	b	c	d	e	f	g	h	i	j	k	l	m
Environment	Extremes of Temperature	14										1			
	Poor Lighting	15										2			
	Vibration	16										2			
	Noise	17										2			
Ergonomic	Working at Heights	18		1				1				1			
	Restricted Workspace	19	1	1							1	1			
	Restricted Identification	20		1			1	1		1		2			
	Restricted Access	21	1	1							1	2			
	Manual Handling	22			1	1				1		2			
Mechanical	Transport	23	1	1								1			
	Hazardous Equipment (also Electrical)	24			1							2			
	Elevated Objects (also Electrical)	25										2			
Security	Sabotage/Vandalism	26										2			
	Trespass	27					1			1		2			
Other	Inconsistent Specification	28										2			
		29													
		30													
		31													
		32													
		33													
		34													
		35													

FIGURE 4.2 - EXAMPLE RISK ASSESSMENT

WORKED EXAMPLE 4.2

STEEL ERECTION

The example of planning for the safe erection of a steel structure is used to demonstrate how design activity and SHE awareness by designers can be used to minimise/mitigate site hazards.

Planning for safe erection

Structural failures can be classified into the following categories:
- Site selection and site development errors - land use planning errors, insufficient or non-existent geotechnical data, unnecessary exposure to natural hazards.
- Programming Deficiencies - unclear or conflicting client expectations, lack of clear definition of scope or intent of project.
- Design errors - in concept, lack of redundancy, load or combination of load not envisaged because of inadequate consideration of construction methods, connection details, calculation errors, misuse of computer software, detailing problems such as incompatible materials or assemblies not constructable, failure to consider maintenance requirements.
- Construction errors - excavation and equipment accidents, improper use of equipment, improper sequencing, inadequate temporary supports, excessive construction/transportation loads, premature removal of formwork, non-conformance to design intent.
- Material deficiencies - material inconsistencies, premature deterioration.
- Operational errors - alterations to structures, change in use, inadequate maintenance.

Planning for the safe erection of a structure should start in the initial design stage with due attention to the human involvement in the erection process and the need to seek practicable and safe methods of working. As design develops, the method should be kept under close and continual review to ensure that there is at least one means of safe erection. The essential elements that need to be considered at each design stage are:

- Stability at all stages of erection
- Effect of erection sequence on stability
- Assessment of structural loadings at all construction stages
- Safe means of connecting components
- Safe handling of components

The Hazard Management Process starts by identifying the SHE critical activities from the method statement, determining the hazards involved and examining ways of preventing the hazards by means of built-in safeguards in the design.

Initial planning and hazard considerations

The following potential hazards should be taken into account.

- Proximity to other activities
- Proximity to other buildings or plant/equipment
- Proximity to overhead or buried services
- Restrictions on access to the site
- Restrictions on space for erection
- Low ground bearing pressures

Design Safeguards - Stability

- Highlight special or unusual stability considerations
- Identify the stage at which the permanent structure is self-supporting and the criteria relied upon for the achievement of this status
- Ensure that any methods used to prevent overturning, collapse or excessive movement during erection do not have a detrimental effect on the permanent structure
- Ensure all realistic load combinations likely to occur during erection have been investigated to determine the most severe instability effects

Design Safeguards - Structural Interconnections

- Design connections to be as simple as possible with suitable devices incorporated to ensure incorrect connections cannot be made

- Ensure sufficient surrounding space to allow safe working and inspection

- Standardise details as far as possible

- Design connections so that as many as possible can be made at ground level

- Incorporate connections in positions where suitable permanent or previously erected features can be utilised to aid safe erection

- Build into the design sufficient tolerances and features to aid safe alignment and initial jointing

- Avoid use, wherever possible, of special connections that involve additional hazards in the erection process

- Build into the design additional features that contribute to safe access and working places such as attachment points for ladders, temporary platforms, guard rails etc.

Design Safeguards - Structural Components

- Design for as many sub-assemblies as possible to be erected at ground level
- Identify dissimilar members uniquely
- Identify centres of gravity or lifting positions

CHAPTER 5

SHE PLAN

5.1 Introduction

The SHE plan, as detailed in this chapter, is intended for use on process/production plant or major building project from feasibility through design and construction to commissioning and handover. Other types of projects e.g. demolition, dismantling and partial development also require a SHE plan.

Whilst the SHE plan is an absolute requirement before construction work starts the contents require information from clients, consultants, architects, designer, Planning Supervisor, Principal Contractor and possibly contractors well before this stage of the project. The plan will subsequently require further development by the Principal Contractor.

For ease of reference most of the figures in this chapter are located at the end of the chapter.

Worked examples describing a process/production plant design risk assessment and HAZCON definition and check sheet are included after the main text.

5.1.1 Who is responsible for providing a plan?

The duty is on the client or agent of the client or developer to ensure that a SHE plan has been prepared for the project before construction phase starts .

The Planning Supervisor appointed by the client, has to ensure a plan is prepared.

5.1.2 Why do you need a plan?

To fulfil the statutory duty.

To ensure tenderers take into account and explain their proposals for managing SHE and clients provide their objectives and background information for the project.

To ensure that all persons involved with the project, client, designers, planning supervisors, Principal Contractors and contractors provide information to the plan and agree to the SHE management controls for health and safety.

To reduce the risk of accidents/incidents both during construction and for the lifetime of the process/production plant.

To reduce the losses associated with accidents /incidents .

To protect the health of all project personnel and subsequent employees.

To reduce pollution and protect the environment.

5.1.3 What is required in the plan?

The plan is required for construction work.

The initial inputs to the plan are from the client, designers, site information sources e.g. site investigations/previous records.

The plan should indicate the client's requirements for any specific approach to be adopted.

The detail will depend on the size and complexity of the project and the contractual arrangements. The main components are safety information from project description, details of risks, safety information from clients/architects/consultants/designers/contractors. These inputs to the plan are to be co-ordinated by the Planning Supervisor for the safety management system.

The designer requirements for specific precautions and highlighting any risk that is covered by specific legislation.

5.1.4   When do you need a plan?

In order for tenderers to take into account the SHE issues the plan will have to be developed within the contract specification.

5.1.5   How does the plan develop?

The responsibility for the plan should be transferred from the Planning Supervisor to the Principal Contractor as soon as the appointment is made. The plan has to be further developed by the Principal Contractor in order to manage the construction phase, see Figure 5.1.

Note:
The client is required to allow sufficient time for the Principal Contractor to develop the plan .

Obviously if design work is still in progress, then further inputs to the plan will be required by the Planning Supervisor.

5.1.6   Main components of a SHE Plan

The main components of the plan are as follows:

*   **Project Summary**
    Objectives
    Management Organisation & Responsibilities
    Programme of Activities
    Existing Environment
    Contract Strategy

*   **Design plan**
    SHE Information
    Organisation and Responsibilities
    Hazard Identification
    Risk Assessment

*   **Procurement Plan**
    Material Hazards
    Construction Risks
    Selection of Principle Contractors

*   **Construction Plan**
    Management Organisation & Responsibilities
    Selection of Contractors
    Site Rules & Procedures
    Welfare Arrangements
    Training
    Hazard Identification/Risk Assessment/Method Statements
    Environmental Control
    Monitoring, Auditing and Review

FIGURE 5.1

PHASES OF A CONSTRUCTION PROJECT

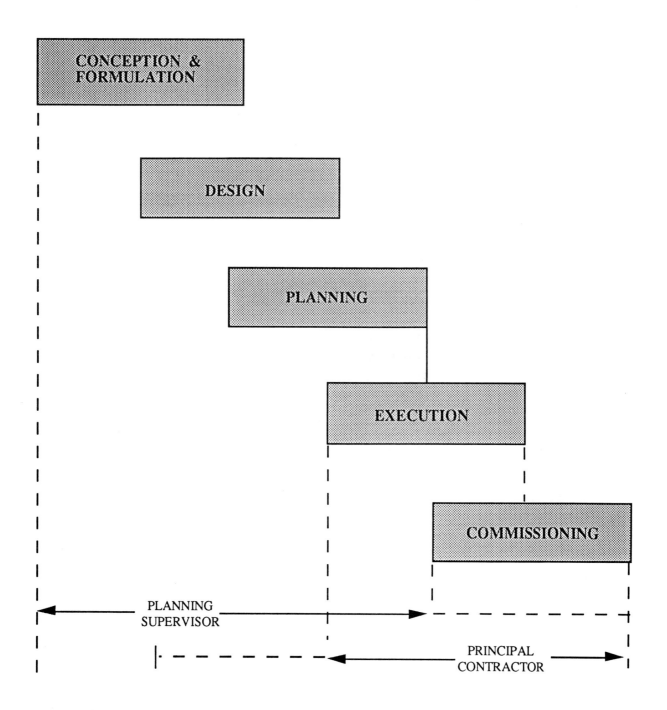

- **Commissioning Plan**
  Pre-Commissioning
  Management Organisation & Responsibilities
  Safety Rules & Procedures
  Training
  Hazard Identification/Risk Assessment/Method Statements
  Environmental Control
  Handover Documents & File
  Monitoring, Auditing and Review

5.2 Project Summary

5.2.1 Objectives

Define the objectives of the project inclusive of SHE considerations.

The client should outline the preferred option for the site with respect to the types of structures, process design parameters with the associated SHE hazard identification and risk assessment for the site based on the general hazards as listed (see also Figure 5.3):

- Environmental
- Geological
- Security
- Biological
- Logistics
- Health
- Chemical
- Electrical
- Mechanical
- Nuclear
- Ergonomics
- Political.
- Legislation.

Legislation, the political influences of the country (e.g. planning, labour, resources and supply routes), although not directly affecting the site works, may influence the arrangements for the site and form the basis for the overall site SHE plan i.e.

Summarise the major constraints highlighted by the general hazard identification/risk assessment. This will confirm the acceptance of these constraints and commitment to managing these risks.

5.2.2 Management Organisation and Responsibilities

The management structure, organisation, policy, responsibilities and communication systems can then be defined to deliver the objectives of the project. Identify client rules regarding the site (e.g. construction/ permit /handover systems).

5.2.3 Programme of Activities

The programme will initially consist of the major activities with respect to design, manufacture, delivery, assembly, construction, testing and commissioning. These major activities will be reduced to the minimum time period required by the overall project time constraints. However durations must take account of the time needed to carry out safety reviews.

Reduction in the time period will be achieved by consideration of manpower resources and material availability. The sequence of activities for the programme will have been decided by the allocated time periods and defined design principles.

It is essential to carry out a constructability analysis using the programme for major activities, (see Figure 5.4). It is essential to include an input from construction engineering either through consultants, client organisations or contractors. This analysis along with the already identified major constraints can be reviewed with respect to the project programme. This review should aim to remove site constraints, minimise site work, identify remaining risks and eliminate hazards. The programme of activities may well require modification of time scale, sequence, construction method or commissioning method.

The project programme should now be an agreed time scale for the major activities. This will have a beneficial effect on the subsidiary activities which make up each major construction activity.

The project programme can be further broken down into detailed activity plans by the Principal Contractor.

5.2.4 Existing Environment

Identify the client's objectives both short term during construction and long term during operation.

Summarise the major constraints highlighted by the general hazard identification/risk assessment. This will confirm the acceptance of these constraints and commitment to managing these risks.

5.2.5 Contract Strategy

The client should define the type of contractual arrangement e.g. "turnkey"/direct managed multi-contract/etc. The management structure, organisation, policy, responsibilities and communication systems can be defined to deliver the objectives of the project.

5.3 Design Plan

5.3.1 Health and Safety Information

The Client is now in a position to supply the Planning Supervisor with safety information from the Project Summary stage as detailed above .

The Planning Supervisor can now commence preparation of SHE file with the project summary information and also supply this information to the designers as the first major input to the SHE plan. The Planning Supervisor has the statutory duty to ensure the designers address the hazards and risks of construction work.

The outline design can now be produced based on the defined standards for the project and client objectives.

5.3.2 Organisation and Responsibilities

The reporting structure, organisation, policy, responsibilities and communication systems can then be defined by the Planning Supervisor to deliver the objectives of the project through the design process. This is essential for interface arrangements between designers of each section of the process/production plant.

5.3.3 Hazard Identification and Risk Assessment

The first priority for designers will be to ensure the safety integrity of the permanent works, process/ production plant and associated machinery. An example flow chart of systematic identification and reduction of risks is shown in Figure 5.5. This assessment is completed by reference to standards, specifications and quantitative risk assessment . It is not intended to detail these methods in this plan but to concentrate on the constructability issues.

The designer can use the hazard and operability analysis, see Figure 5.6, to assist in proving the adequacy of the design. Although this is based on the final operation method of the plant it will have a useful input into the identification of hazards especially as regards commissioning .

Design for construction has to address the layout and movement of materials, machinery and resources along with the method and sequence of construction activities. The method of proving the operation of the process/production plant design parameters. The management and maintenance of the facility and finally the decommissioning /demolition of the facility. The designer is in a position to influence SHE on site in the following activities:

- Access:
  - To the site by external sources to deliver, off load, collect and dispose of materials.

  - Across the site to permit safe transportation of materials to and from the working area.
    To and across the site for service personnel to maintain, repair, inspect, during the construction process.

  - Plant separation distances during construction safety, maintenance activities and the operation of contingency plans.

- Methods:
  - Constructing the plant /process components.
  - Sequence for commissioning /handover of the process /plant
  - Maintaining and managing the facility
  - Decommissioning and demolition of the process /plant components.

The safest option for controlling the identified risks can be decided by the Planning Supervisor. The Planning Supervisor has to co-ordinate the health and safety aspects of design and planning.

The designer may in the course of the above analysis provide a number of options which have to be reviewed by the Planning Supervisor with respect to project health and safety objectives. As the decision may affect the overall technical and financial objectives of the project then the client will have to agree to the level of residual risk.

This process will also be required for:
The design for commissioning/handover, maintaining and managing the facility, decommissioning and demolition.

5.4 Procurement Plan

The Planning Supervisor will have to ensure the co-ordination of the construction material process to provide an input to the SHE plan which eliminates or reduces risk to the construction, maintenance, dismantling and demolition personnel and environment.

5.4.1 Material Hazards

The health and environment of the construction maintenance dismantling and demolition personnel can be adversely affected by procurement specifications. Therefore the classification of materials must be known from data sheets the associated risks along with the measures required for control of those risks. The procurement process should address the required use of hazardous material and ensure the relevant assessment (Control of Substances Hazardous to Health Assessment is acceptable. This review should address not only the SHE requirements but project costs in storage, use, disposal and possible inadvertent emissions/discharges, affects on programme time, resources and equipment.

5.4.2 Construction Risks

The supply of equipment which requires complex assembly or site manufacturing will require an assessment as to the possible increased safety problems.

The use of hazardous materials creates additional safety problems for the Principal Contractor both in the provision of personal protective equipment, protection of other contractors working adjacent the area of risk, often an increased fire risk associated with storage, use and waste. The spillage, emission of hazardous substances can also create environment risks both to contractors and to the public. Special health surveillance may be required along with additional training and de-contamination equipment.

5.4.3 Supply and Install Contracts

These types of contract are often outside of the main project process either because of specialist equipment or direct issue by the client. The Planning Supervisor has to ensure that all such contracts involving design material procurement, construction and commissioning are included as an input to the SHE plan.

5.4.4 Selection of Principal Contractor

The existing selection criteria has to be reinforced as regards the management ability of the contractor to fulfil this role.

5.5 Construction Plan

The construction phase commences with the clients /designers overall objectives for the plant/structure. The Principal Contractor is immediately constrained as regards material costs, resources permitted, completion date, physical and environmental limits. The Principal Contractor will be required to provide the construction methodology, (in situ, pre-assembly, off-site, fabrication etc.), range and type of sub-contractors.

The Principal Contractor should develop the plan for the site:

5.5.1 Management and Organisation

The Principal Contractor has a critical role in deciding the priorities for the construction work. The SHE plan will have already defined the sequence of activities but the principle contractor will be aware of the proposed and current site activities and possible interface problems which could be present at this stage of the project.

This has to identify the major constraints for the project (e.g. physical and environmental), some of which will have been already 'flagged' in the plan by the Planning Supervisor.

Define the management responsibilities to control and monitor safety and incorporate the approach to be adopted for SHE management.

The system of reporting the SHE information to the Principal Contractor to incorporate in the SHE Plan and the retention of information in the SHE File for the project.

The continuing requirement to consider all activities across the site including those outside or crossing the project boundary. The interface requirements with the client across the site and liaison with the public and statutory bodies.

5.5.2 Selection of Contractors

Arrangements for pre-qualification, selection and approval of contractors prior to tenders.

5.5.3 Site Rules and Procedures

The control of site activities related to managing SHE for all contractors across the site, including:

- Site regulations/rules.
- Traffic control, site office accommodation, storage of material, emergency procedures , fire plan welfare facilities, first aid.
- The safety rule system to be used in connection with live systems.
- The safety rule system to be used for work not on live systems e.g. excavation, welding burning access to non operational areas.
- Arrangements for monitoring and reviewing health and safety compliance.
- The requirements for the reporting of accident statistics.

5.5.4 Health Arrangements

- Arrangements for ensuring all site personnel are medically fit for work.
- The control of first aid facilities.

5.5.5 Hazard Identification /Risk Assessment/Method Statements

In carrying out hazard identification and risk assessment of the detailed work activities all contractors must provide the method of reducing the risks (e.g. method statement alternative installation method which should be assessed as the original design). If alternative methods are proposed then reference to the Planning Supervisor/Principal Contractor can ensure any design co-ordination is completed.

5.5.6 Risk assessment for construction work

There are a number of good examples of risk assessment systems including those given in Figures 5.7, 5.8, 5.9, 5.10.

5.5.7 Project Method Statements

The activities already identified by the designer as high risk will also require the Principal Contractor to provide or obtain method statements.

The method statement for a work package should be in sufficient detail to provide the correct sequence of work a description of all the activities so that he supervisor can use it to manage the work. The method statement should highlight the preparation of safety equipment (e.g. PPE, access systems, mobile plant, and work equipment), along with reference to other assessment such as manual handling, Noise and COSHH.

The contractor has to provide information on the implementation of the SHE plan, in a form which is easily retrievable by the Principal Contractor. Therefore it is incumbent on the Principal Contractor to ensure that all contractors deliver their input to the plan and, in particular, the agreed method of work. The provision of the contents of a method statement should be formally signed on to by construction personnel to verify the training and information process.

It is often the case that small contractors for minor activities - which nevertheless have a high risk - are unable to produce written method statements or the time to carry out the work leaves insufficient time to produce such method statements. Such work should never be allowed to commence without a clear indication of the methods of work, otherwise there will be no indication that the contractor has prepared all the safety equipment for the work.

The attached pro-forma (see Figures 5.11, 5.12 and 5.13) can be used as a formal method statement by asking all the questions on the check sheet. This way the contractor is committed to the agreed method of work as the pro-forma requires signing by both parties. This is, of course, time consuming and should only be used as the minimum level of work control for site work.

5.5.8   Training

The Principal Contractor must ensure that arrangements are in place for assessing the level of safety training achieved by employees for the particular work skills such as:
* riggers trained in the safety of lifting equipment
* the induction training requirements for the site
* the arrangements for on site training (e.g. toolbox talks, publicity and manufacturers instructions).

5.5.9   Environmental Control

The Principal Contractor is responsible for ensuring that the following are in place:

* Arrangements for delivery , storage , distribution and disposal across the site.

* Identification of waste disposal routes and control procedures. The preparation of a contingency plan and identification of the equipment for implementation of the plan.

* Noise assessment across the site and especially the perimeter areas.

* Methods of ensuring all discharges to drains, emissions to atmosphere are monitored to ensure compliance with the environmental consents.

5.5.10   Monitoring, Auditing and Review

The Principal Contractor is required to monitor compliance with the SHE plan. This will include the following:

* Audit the contents of method statements.

* Communicate safety information (e.g. safety meetings , notice boards, co-ordination meetings between contractors and sub- contractors, method statement meetings).

* Implement site safety monitoring during the daily work on site , the persons to carry out safety inspections across the site and the persons to audit of the management systems as well as the site works.

* Review all accidents and incidents as to remedial action.

5.6   Commissioning Plan

5.6.1   Pre-Commissioning

The pre-commissioning work may commence whilst construction work is still in progress and when partial or temporary supply systems are available. The pre-commissioning work may involve checking of systems without supplies available or process fluids/gases.

5.6.2   Commissioning

The SHE plan will require the safety information as described:

- **Management and Organisation**

Description of management responsibilities to control and monitor safety, this may be a combination of the client management and operating personnel, principle contractor or other contractors.

The system of reporting the SHE information to the responsible person for the plan and the retention of this information in the SHE File for the project.

- **Safety Rules and Procedures**

The control of activities related to managing SHE for all commissioning and the protection of personnel across the site e.g. site regulations/rules, hazard identification and risk assessment, storage of materials, emergency procedures, fire plan, welfare facilities, first aid and contingency plan. The safety rule system to be used in connection with live systems. The construction contractor is immediately constrained as regards completion date, physical and environmental limits.

- **Training**

Arrangements for assessing the level of safety training achieved by employees for the particular commissioning procedure. Verification of the contingency, emergency, fire procedures. The induction training requirements for the site.

- **Hazard Identification/Risk Assessment/Commissioning Procedures**

The designer will have already carried out the assessment of the commissioning procedure, and highlighted where the high risk areas are in commissioning/handover.

The designer is the only person who can define the exact requirements for commissioning to achieve the design specification operating parameters. The detail of such activities may have to be broken down by the Principle Contractor/Commissioning engineer to carry out a hazard analysis and operability study for commissioning work.

In carrying out hazard identification and risk assessment of the detailed commissioning procedures the Principal Contractor must provide the method of reducing the risks (e.g. method statement), which should be assessed as the original design intent. The commissioning procedure should highlight the preparation of safety equipment (e.g. PPE, access systems, mobile plant, and work equipment), along with reference to other assessment such as manual handling, noise and COSHH.

- **Method Statements**

The commissioning procedure may require additional detail in the form of a method statement to provide the correct sequence of work a description of all the activities so that the Principal Contractor can use it to manage the work.

- **Environmental Control**

Arrangements for delivery, storage, distribution and disposal across the site.

The identification of waste disposal routes and control procedures.

The preparation of a contingency plan and identification of the equipment for implementation of the plan.

The responsibilities for noise assessment across the site and especially the perimeter areas.

The method of ensuring all discharges to drains, emissions to atmosphere are monitored to ensure compliance with the environmental consents.

•   **Monitoring, Auditing and Review**

The communication of safety information (e.g. safety meetings, notice boards, co-ordination meetings between contractors and sub- contractors).

The persons to carry out site safety monitoring during the daily work on site, the persons to carry out safety inspections across the site and the persons to carry out auditing of the management systems as well as the site works.

•   **Handover Documents and File**

This process is often in stages due to contractual arrangements but on final completion the the Planning Supervisor has to ensure the SHE File is provided for the client and contains all relevant documents.

WORKED EXAMPLE 5.1

PROCESS/PRODUCTION PLANT DESIGN RISK ASSESSMENT

Process/production plant construction.

In order to assist in co-ordinating the design process and provide a structured approach to hazard identification and risk assessment for construction of a process/production plant the following of a matrix system has been adapted for use by designers. In order to allow such analysis the process /production plant has been separated into the following sections: See Figure 5.2.

- Material input process
- Conversion/ manufacturing process
- Services input systems
- Waste/emission systems
- Output systems

These sections are common to all process/production plants. The designer would, of course, have to consider the whole process as regards the technical safety of the process.

But the majority of process plants are constructed and commissioned in sections and connected together for final complete handover commissioning.

Process/Production Plant Systems
Hazard identification/risk assessment of design

For each major process system an assessment of design can be completed.
For example:

- Plant /Production Material Input Process
- Plant/Process/Conversion/Manufacturing Process
- Plant/Production Services input systems
- Plant/Production Waste/Emission Systems
- Plant/Production Output Systems

The hazard category list is listed below and can be broken down into further detail as required for each type of project:

Hazard Categorisation

Physical (P):   Hydrocarbons Under Pressure
High Pressure Liquids or Gas
Operations in Water
High temperature or Cryogenic Fluids
Hazardous Surfaces
Ignition Sources

Chemical(C):   Explosive
Explosive Gas Generators
Ignition Sources

Electrical(E):   Ignition Sources
Hazardous Equipment
Electrical energy

Biological(B):   Toxic Substances
Biological Hazards
Asphyxiating Atmospheres

Figure 5.2

Process/Production Plant Construction

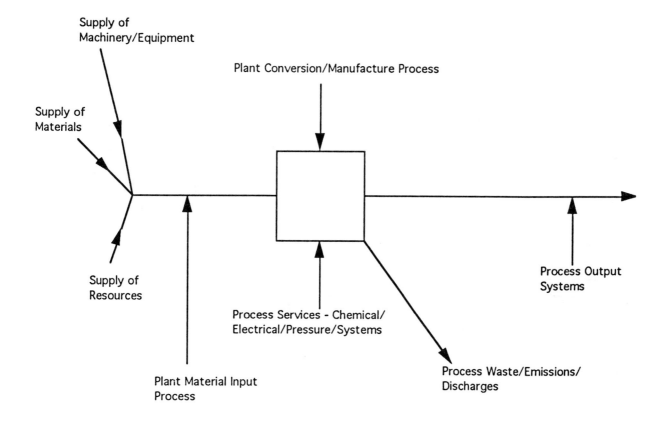

Source: Dave Tubb, PowerGen

Environmental(EN):Ground Conditions

Ergonomic(ERG):   Elevated Objects
                    Working at Height
                    Hazardous Surfaces

Mechanical(M):   Transport
                    Hazardous Equipment
                    Elevated Objects

Security(S):   Public Access

Example of Design Hazard/Risk Assessment: Material Input Process

PARAMETERS	HAZARDS								RISK	
	P	C	E	H	B	EN	ERG	M	LOW	HIGH
Material										
Access										
Supply Route										
Position										
Ground Condition										
Contingency Systems										
Storage Facilities										
Maintenance Facilities										

**Example of Design Hazard/Risk Assessment: e.g.
Plant/Production/Manufacture/Conversion Process**

	HAZARDS									RISK	
	P	C	E	H	B	EN	ERG	M	S	LOW	HIGH
ACTIVITY											
Excavation											
Foundation											
Support Structure											
Interior Finish											
Mechanical Installation											
H&V Installation											
Painting											
Instrument Installation											
Communication Systems											
Fire Protection Installation											

Once a high risk category has been identified for a particular activity then it is for the designer to supply the information on how the risk can be eliminated, reduced by the design. The scope for pre-assembly or modular approach is an important consideration to reduce the site risks.
If the risk cannot be eliminated or reduced by design then a construction management procedure may be required to be developed by the Principal Contractor to control the risk.

WORKED EXAMPLE 5.2

HAZCON DEFINITION AND CHECKLIST

Definition of HAZCON

A formal procedure developed by one company for early identification and assessment of safety, occupational health and environmental (SHE) hazards in building operations and works of engineering construction to enable all reasonably practical steps to be taken to reduce or eliminate the risk.

HAZCON 1 (See Figure 5.3)

HAZCON 1 is carried out to identify major hazards to client personnel, contractors, visitors, or general public - (applying inside or outside the site boundary) together with actions/recommendations for hazard elimination or reduction. It uses checklists as an aide memoire and is carried out as early as possible in the project but in any case before the project scope and site are fixed.

HAZCON 2 (See Figure 5.4)

HAZCON 2 is carried out to provide a detailed assessment of construction hazards based on the completion of a significant level of engineering definition but at least including plans and elevation together with draft overall construction method statement, contract plan, project programme and site layout drawings. It should also include a review of HAZCON 1 results to see whether the development of the scope of the project has added or removed any major construction hazards.

Figure 5.3

HAZCON 1 CHECKLIST

Project Title			
Project Number	Date	Tick if applicable	
Factors to be considered during Construction		Within the works	Outside the works
ENVIRONMENT			
Contaminated Ground			
Unstable Ground			
Existing Underground Services			
Access Routes - Vehicles, Personnel, Emergency			
Climatic Conditions - Cold, Heat, Rain, Lightning, Darkness			
Cultural Factors			
Waste Disposal			
IDENTIFY MAJOR RISK FACTORS			
Work At Height			
Work Over Water			
Work in Confined Spaces			
Very Large Lifting Operations			
IDENTIFY MAJOR RISK SUBSTANCES			
Lead			
Asbestos			
Radiochemicals			
PCB's			
Flammables			
Other			
RISKS TO EXISTING FACILITIES ARISING FROM CONSTRUCITON WORK			
Noises/Disturbance			
Vibration			
Emissions			
Fire			
RISKS TO CONSTRUCTION WORK ARISING FROM EXISTING FACILITIES			
Explosion			
Fire			
Emissions			
Electromagnetic Radiation			
Chemical Contamination			
Biological Risks			
RISKS AT COSTRUCTION/COMMISSIONING INTERFACE			
Testing			
Phased Handover			
Fumigation			
Author:			

Figure 5.4

HAZCON 2 CHECKLIST

A. SUMMARY OF TOPICS

1. Review HAZCON 1 report.

2. Review "site establishment safety planner" (Company in-house planning check).

3. Review draft overall method statement.

4. Review project programme.

5. Review selected drawings (plan and elevations).

6. Review Draft Contract Plan and safety requirements to be included in site contracts.

7. Discuss effects of site constraints.

8. Discuss options for minimising scope of site work.

9. Discuss testing, pre-commissioning, commissioning and eventual demolition.

10. a)   Write-up recommendation for alterations to:
    - overall method statement
    - contract plan
    - programme
    - design
    - scope of site work

    b)   Assess remaining risks and document actions required to reduce them.

11. Confirm method for the following up of recommendations.

Figure 5.5

Flow Chart for Systematic Identification and Reduction of Risks

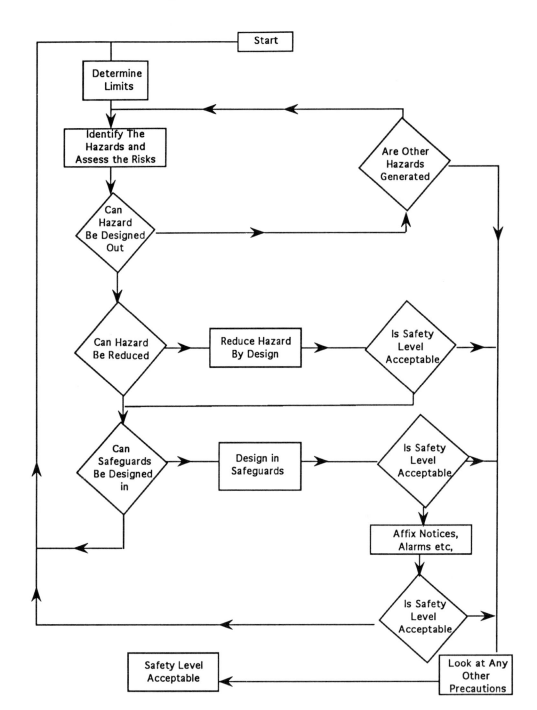

When making the decision on whether the safety level is adequate, the designer must be sure that the intended level of safety has been reached, does not prevent the process/production plant and associated machinery from performing its intended function and does not generate other hazards.

Source: A Guide to European Machinery Safety Standards. Pils GmbH & Co. 1993. p.57.

Figure 5.6

HAZOP TECHNIQUE

The examination procedure uses a series of questions based on guide words to test the integrity of each part of the design to every theoretical deviation.

This results in a number of possible causes, and their operational consequences and leads to actions required for safeguarding the plant and the personnel involved before commissioning of the plant commences.

Although the report from such a HAZOP review may be time-consuming to produce, the actual process of asking and arriving at a suitable response is easily achieved, assuming the panel contains the appropriate persons with authority to make such decisions.

This HAZOP study may differ slightly from the original design HAZOP because of the piecemeal way the process plant or structure systems are commissioned.

TABLE OF GUIDE WORDS

Guide Word	Deviations	Possible Causes	Consequences	Action
None	No flow, quantity, temperature pressure etc. when there should be			
Reverse	Opposite effect to design intention			
More	Increase in flow, quantity, temperature, pressure, current, voltage, radiation compared with design			
Less	Decrease in flow, quantity, temperature, pressure, current, voltage, radiation compared with design			
Part of	Change in the composition of the system, component ratio change, component missing			
As Well As	Additions to the composition of the system, contamination, moisture, vapour, viscosity			
Other Than	Changes form normal operation start-up, shutdown, uprating, low rate running, alternative operation mode, failure of plant services, maintenance			

The guide words above are broadly used, and when applied to the plant items, it is often necessary to use them in conjunction with the term of a physical property. But this process can also be used for the protection of personnel as the guide word and the deviation as one of the properties shown below.

Examples of such properties that it may be useful to consider are:
   Flow, Pressure, Temperature, Capacity, Quantity, Viscosity, Moisture, Contamination, Force, Radioactivity.

Protection of Personnel:
   Access, Training, Procedures, Personal Protection, Communications.

Figure 5.7

RISK ASSESSMENT FORM HSC1

OPERATION:

LOCATION:

PERSONNEL INVOLVED:

HAZARD	RISK (see over for key)			
	L	M	H	COMMENTS
FALLS OF PERSONS				
FALLS OF MATERIALS				
MANUAL HANDLING				
STEPPING ON/STRIKING OBJECTS				
TRAPPING				
HAND TOOLS				
MECHANICAL EQUIPMENT				
ELECTRICAL				
HARMFUL SUBSTANCES				
FIRE				
EXPLOSION				
TRANSPORTING INC. MOBILE CRANES				
CONFINED SPACES				
WORKING AT HEIGHTS				
EXCAVATIONS				
OTHER (specify)				

PRIORITISE RISK   INSIGNIFICANT - LOW - MEDIUM - HIGH
(If insignificant - no further action)

NEXT STEP   SAFE SYSTEM OF WORK - PROCEDURE!
IS THERE A METHOD STATEMENT?

ACTIONS

SIGNED: ....   DATED: ....

Source: ECIA

Figure 5.8

RISK ASSESSMENT SUMMARY PART 1				Ref. No. *example*	
Site: *example*			Location: *example*		

Persons exposed	√	Comments (include reference to disabled, trainees, etc.			
Employees	√	*Access to plant room restricted to authorised persons*			
Other workers	x				
Public	x				

Hazards Identified   x if present/requiring control   √ if absent/not significant

Physical Injury Hazards		Physical Agents		Manual Handling	
Mobile Plant	√	Ionising Radiation	√	Manual Handling Injury	√
Moving parts of machine	x	Lasers	√		
Moving Materials	√	Ultraviolet Light	√	Miscellaneous	
Falls from heights	√	Cold Objects	√	Weather	√
Access Equipment	√	Hot Objects	√	Lone Working	√
Slips, Trips, Falls	√	Temperature	√	Confined Spaces	√
Excavations	√	Noise/Vibration	√	Restricted Access	√
Pressurised Systems	√	Hazardous Substances	√		
Electrical	x	Hazardous Substances	x	Other - Communications	x
Hot Work/Fire	√	Micro-organisms	√	Other	√
Explosion	√	Vermin/Weil's Disease	√	Other	√

If Other (specify) *Need to agree with client the shutting down of system*

....

Specific Site Conditions
Describe site elements which create specific risks (i.e. weather conditions for roof work, etc.)
which require precautions to be taken during works:
*Internal plant room, not applicable except agreement to used lift out of normal working hours to get new
pump to 5th floor, and old pump down.*

....

....

Risk Evaluation (see checklist above)

Score 1 2 3 Unlikely/Possible/ Likely/Minor/ Moderate/Serious	Likelihood of Harm Score 1 - 3		Severity Score 1 - 3		Risk Number Scores multiplied
Physical Injury	*Likely*	*- 3*	*Moderate*	*- 2*	3 x 2 = 6
Physical Agents	*Unlikely*	*- 1*	*Minor*	*- 1*	1 x 1 = 1
Hazardous Substances	*Possible*	*- 2*	*Minor*	*- 1*	2 x 1 = 2
Manual Handling	*Likely*	*- 3*	*Moderate*	*- 2*	3 x 2 = 6
Miscellaneous	*Unlikely*	*- 1*	*Minor*	*- 1*	1 x 1 = 1

State Key Risks (Use risk evaluation score for priorities - 5+ priorities)
Back strain - pump weighs 60kg
Foot injury - if pump slips and is dropped on foot
Pump to be isolated before working or risk of electrical accident
Pump to be isolated before working or risk of exposure to feed material

Control Measure - See Risk Assessment Summary Form 2 attached

Signed ....J Smith ....   Date ......1/7/93 ....

Position ....Foreman ....

DON'T FORGET TO MONITOR AND REASSESS

Source: HVCA

Figure 5.9

RISK ASSESSMENT SUMMARY PART 2		Ref.No. *example*
Site: *examples*		Location: *anywhere*
Assessment for *Changing a pump in a plant room* Significant risks: *Back strain, Foot injury, Electrical, spillage/contamination (skin)*		
CONTRACT ITEM	**DETAILS OF CONTROL MEASURES**	
Documents Procedures etc.	*Company Procedure on competency of site staff Standard procedure for documenting plant maintenance for clients (site log).*	
Information	*Operatives advised of risks of back strain injuries, foot injuries, electrical hazard and exposure to materials in system.*	
Instruction	*Follow standard procedures for pump change including isolation, working in team of 2 (heavy pump).*	
Training	*Induction for all operatives. Manual handling - briefing on safe techniques.*	
Supervision	*Supervisor to check that operatives have equipment required, aware of need for isolation of pump before commencing work.*	
Access	*Access to plant room should be safe. Use of lift.*	
Environment	*Lighting poor, additional to be taken on site. If air handling plant running, noisy area requiring hearing defenders.*	
Equipment	*Trolley to be used to move pumps. Tripod hoist may be used to swing pump out of/into position if required.*	
Emergencies	*Standard site first aid, fire protection, evacuation, accident reporting and investigation.*	
Communications	*Operatives to advise client before shutting down system containing pump.*	
COSHH	*Operatives given COSHH Assessment for grease. Rubber gloves to be worn when old pump removed, in case of spillage, and spillage to be cleaned up using Spillsorb.*	
PPE	*Safety shoes/boots to be worn, gloves (see COSHH) and hearing defenders (Standard Issue Muff) if required (see environment above).*	
Other Procedures	*Pump to be electrically isolated and locked off before work commences. Valves each side of pump to be closed prior to commencement, and reopened when new pump in place.*	

The above controls have been selected to protect the health and safety of operatives and others who may be affected by the work. The controls have been designed to protect against the risks recorded on Risk Assessment Summary Part 1. This general guidance should only be used when it is appropriate to specific site specifications.

Source: HVCA

Figure 5.10

Project General Risk Assessment

Project .... Date ....

Note: Complete a separate sheet for each operation/activity

Left Section							Right Section	YES	NO
OPERATION/ACTIVITY							Mobile Scaffold		
							Scaffolding		
							Lifting Attachments		
LOCATION: GROUND/BELOW/ABOVE							Mechanical Hoist		
SITE AREA:							Cradle		
R1. Potential severity of INJURY or Illness	1	2	3	4	5		Power Platforms		
							Excavation Shoring		
1. Minor 2. Major - one person 3. Major Multiple 4. Fatal - one person 5. Multiple Fatal							Task Lighting		
R2. Number of workers exposed to hazard	1	2	3	4	5		Ventilation Extraction Equipment		
1.1 2. 2 to 10 3. 11 to 50 4. 51 to 100 5. 101							Waste Skips		
R3. Probability of Injury or Illness (	1	2	3	4	5		Excavators		
1. Improbable 2. Possible 3. Occasional 4. Regular Occurrence 5. Common Occurrence							PERSONAL PROTECTIVE EQUIPMENT (PPE)	YES	NO
RISK RATING = R1 X R2 X R3							Hard Hat		
PLEASE COMPLETE THE FOLLOWING CHECKLIST FOR HAZARDS /EQUIPMENT/PPE/ TOOLS/MATERIALS							Protective Footwear		
HAZARDS	YES	NO					Eye Protection		
Stepping on, Striking against							Face Visor		
Manual Handling							Gloves		
Hand Tools Mechanical							Overalls		
Excavations							Hearing Protection		
Lifting Equipment							Safety Harness		
Machinery							Securing Points for Safety Harness		
Fall on flat							Respirator		
Fall - ladders, scaffolding/towers							Breathing Apparatus		
Fall - holes, exposed edges							First Aid Equipment		
Fall - Others							Fire Precaution		
Falls of Materials							TOOLS/MATERIALS	YES	NO
Electrical							Trade Tools		
COSHH							Test Equipment		
Noise							Cable Detector		
							Rescue Equipment		
Asbestos							Lifting Slings		
3rd Party (public/contractor)							Explosives		
Overhead power lines							Chains		
Power Tools - Electrical							Fibre Monitor		
Power Tools - Pneumatic							EXTRA CONTROL, MEASURES PROTECTION OR SUPERVISOR NEEDED IN VIEW OF WORK		
Drowning							Waste Control		
Underground Services							Warning Signs Displayed		
Dust							Barriers Provided		
Fire							Comply with Permit System		
Radiation							Supervisor check area		
Vibration							Special Training		
Temperature							Competency Certificate		
EQUIPMENT NECESSARY	YES	NO					Clear and safe access		
Ladder							Safety Man/Assistant		
Steps/Trestles							Method Statement		
							Site Pre-work meeting		

ASSESSMENT SIGNATURE .... ASSESSMENT DATE ....

Source: PowerGen

Figure 5.11

PROJECT _____

SUBJECT: SUB-CONTRACTORS SAFE SYSTEM OF WORK (METHOD STATEMENT)

SUB-CONTRACTOR _____ TRADE _____

DATE _____

BRIEF DESCRIPTION OF THE WORK

LIST YOUR SEQUENCE OF OPERATIONS

1. _____   6. _____

2. _____   7. _____

3. _____   8. _____

4. _____   9. _____

5. _____   10. _____

MANAGEMENT STRUCTURE

- VISITING MANAGER   _____

- SITE SUPERVISOR   _____

- WHO IS RESPONSIBLE FOR SAFETY   _____

- OUT OF HOURS CONTACT NAME   _____

- OUT OF HOURS PHONE No   _____

- WHO CHECKS THE WORK   _____

- IS THERE A CHECK SHEET   _____

SAFETY AND OPERATIONS DETAILS: DELETE/ADD AS REQUIRED

IS A PERMIT TO WORK REQUIRED - EXCAVATION/DEMOLITION/HOT WORK/CONFINED SPACES/
                               LIVE MANHOLES/LIFT SHAFTS/WORK OUTSIDE THE SITE/
                               PLANT or SWITCH ROOMS

ARE EXISTING SERVICES IN THE   - ELECTRICITY/GAS/WATER/BT/COMPUTER
AREA

IF YES, STATE PRECAUTIONS

	Page: 1 out of 3

Reproduced with the kind permission of John Laing Construction

Figure 5.12

ARE THERE EXISTING HAZARDS IN THE WORK AREA IF YES, STATE PRECAUTIONS	- ASBESTOS/LEAD PAINT/CHEMICALS/RADIATION - CONTAMINATED LAND/UNDERGROUND DUCT OR FOUNDATIONS/SHAFTS/TANKS
HOW WILL YOURN OPERATIVES GAIN ACCESS TO THEIR PLACE OF WORK	- GROUND LEVEL/LADDER/SCAFFOLD/STAIRS
WHAT WILL YOUR OPERATIVES USE AS A WORKING PLATFORM	- GUARDRAIL/HARNESS/NET/PARAPET/STATE ANY OTHER:
WHAT PROTECTIVE EQUIPMENT WILL BE PROVIDED	- HELMET/GLOVES/MASKS/GOGGLES/W.PROOFS/RESPIRATORS/FOOTWEAR
WHAT OTHER SAFETY EQUIPMENT WILL BE PROVIDED	
HOW WILL THE PUBLIC OR OTHER TRADES BE PROTECTED	- HOARDINGS/BARRIERS/FENCING/SIGNS/LIGHTS/BRICK GUARDS
HOW IS THE MATERIAL TO BE FIXED OR CUT OR DRILLED	- NAILED/SCREWED/SHOTFIRED/WELDED/GLUED/SPRAYED/BRUSHED/SAWN/DRILLED/BOLTED STATE OTHER:
DOES FIXING/APPLICATION EQUIPMENT REQUIRE A TEST CERTIFICATE OR TRAINING	- IF YES, GIVE DETAILS
WHAT PLANT WILL BE USED	- EXCAVATOR/FORKLIFT/DUMPER/MIXER/HOIST/MOBILE WORK PLATFORM
DOES THE PLANT/EQUIPMENT REQUIRE TEST CERTIFICATES OR OPERATOR TRAINING	- IF YES, GIVE DETAILS
TRANSPORT TO SITE CONSIDERATIONS	- WIDE LOAD/POLICE ESCORT/NOTICES
SPECIAL SITE ACCESS REQUIREMENTS	- HARDSTANDING/USE OF TEMPORARY ROADS/RAMPS
MATERIAL PACKING DETAILS	- PALLETS/SHRINK WRAPPING/BOXES/TINS/DRUMS
MATERIAL STORAGE DETAILS	- COVERED/UNCOVERED/STORED/CONTROLLED/SECURED
METHOD OF UNLOADING	- HYAB/MOBILE CRANE/FORKLIFT/MANUALLY

	Page: 2 out of 3

Reproduced with the kind permission of John Laing Construction

Total Project Management

Figure 5.13

SITE DISTRIBUTION DETAILS — MANUALLY/FORKLIFT/EXCAVATOR

DISTRIBUTION IN BUILDING — MANUAL/FORKLIFT/PALLET TRUCK/BARROW

HOISE/LIFT INTO POSITION — HOISE/FORKLIFT/CRANE/MANUAL/WINCH

ARE COSHH ASSESSMENTS REQUIRED

PROECTION OF MATERIAL — HARDBOARD/PLY/PLASTIC/PAPER/TAPE/ TARPAULIN

HOW DO YOU INTEND TO MINIMISE THE FOLLOWING HAZARDS?

- NOISE _____
- DUST _____
- EXCESS WATER _____
- ODOUR/FUMES _____
- EXHAUST FUMES _____
- OTHER _____

WHAT TEMPORARY SERVICES ARE REQUIRED?

- POWER _____ BY _____
- LIGHTING _____ BY _____
- WATER _____ BY _____
- OTHER _____ BY _____

ARE THERE TEMPORARY WORKS (i.e. TRENCH SUPPORT/SHEET/PILES/BRACING)
IF YES PLEASE GIVE DETAILS

IS THERE ANY FALSEWORK (i.e. FORMWORK/DECKING/MOULDS/CASINGS)
IF YES PLEASE GIVE DETAILS

GIVE DETAILS OF SETTING OUT - BY   / BY SUBCONTRACTOR

STATE OTHER RELEVANT INSTALLATION DETAILS/METHODS

THIS METHOD STATEMENT IS TO BE READ, UNDERSTOOD AND SIGNED BY ALL INVOLVED.
A COPY IS TO BE RETAINED, ON SITE, BY THE SUB-CONTRACTORS SUPERVISOR:

NAME   SIGNATURE   POSITION/TRADE   DATE

MONITORED BY: SIGNED   DATE

IS A MORE DETAILED METHOD STATEMENT REQUIRED   YES | NO   IF YES SPECIFY

	Page: 2 out of 3

Reproduced with the kind permission of John Laing Construction

80

Figure 5.14

DESIGN ENGINEERING STANDARD		NUMBER :		
		ISSUE DATE :		
		PAGE :		

TITLE: DESIGN PROCEDURE - CIVIL SAFETY CHECKLIST

SAFETY ITEM	YES	NO	NOT APPL	ACTION REQUIRED AND/OR REMARKS	REV
1. GENERAL					
1.1 Have the following fire and/or explosion hazards been considered?					
a. Gas					
b. Liquid					
c. Dust					
d. Solid					
1.2 Have hazards of chemicals, toxicological radioactive, and reactive properties of materials been considered?					
1.3 Have special safety precautions required for process (such as environmental hazards) been considered?					
1.4 Have earthquake forces been considered					
1.5 Have slipping hazards of dust been considered?					
2. PLANT LAYOUT					
2.1 Has the required access for cranes, fire trucks and ambulances been provided?					
2.2 Have the required multiple exits (in opposite directions) for evacuation of personnel been provided?					
a. No 'dead-end' areas?					
b. Barriers provided at secondary entrances to the plant?					
c. Are there 2 exists from control room, MCC room, other rooms?					
d. Are escape ladders provided from roofs and pits?					
2.3 Have walking right-of-ways been respected?					
a. Access and escape routes free from obstructions?					
b. Doors or windows not projecting into walkways when open?					

Source: Dow Europe

Figure 5.15

DEPARTMENTAL GUIDE
PIPING DESIGN

	SAFETY CHECKLIST				
	DESCRIPTION/QUESTION	YES	NO	N/A	REMARKS/ACTION
1.	GENERAL				
1.1	Are there any safety requirements from the client available (scope)?				
1.2	Is a safety checklist from the client available specifically for the job?				
1.3	Is this LCV safety checklist applicable for the job?				
1.4	Is a job safety requirement list/document available?				
1.5	Are model reviews scheduled for this job?				
1.6	Are the piping specifications approved by the Material Engineering group?				
1.7	Are the piping material specifications well defined on the P&I diagrams?				
1.8	Is an approved line schedule available with temperatures, pressures and insulation/tracing?				
1.9	Are the critical lines indicated?				
1.10	Does the line schedule have the same revision as the P&I diagram?				
1.11	Are the critical lines approved by the Stress section?				
1.12	Are the critical lines approved by the Process section?				
1.13	Are the remarks from the Stress and Process sections implemented in the design?				

Source: ABB Lummus Crest B.V.

Figure 5.16

DEPARTMENTAL GUIDE
CIVIL/STRUCTURAL

SAFETY CHECKLIST					
	DESCRIPTION/QUESTION	YES	NO	N/A	REMARKS/ACTION
1.	GENERAL				
1.1	Are there any SHE requirements from the client available (e.g. safety checklist)?				
1.2	Has LCV prepared project specific standards procedures/practices/specifications?				
1.3	Has a site visit been planned?				
1.4	Are clients requirements with respect to site visit available?				
1.5	Is reliable as-built information available?				
1.6	Are authority SHE requirements defined and available? • Building approval (BoWoTo) • Environmental approval (e.g. DCMR) - Emissions to atmosphere - Emissions to water - Emissions to spoil - Noise/vibrations - Waste transportation - Disposal of contaminated materials • Requirements for working environment (ARBO0 • Requirements for ergonomics				
2.	PLANT LAYOUT				
2.1	Are reliable meteorological data available?				

Source: ABB Lummus Crest B.V.

CHAPTER 6

SHE COSTS AND BENEFITS

6.1   Introduction

This chapter looks at the costs and benefits of SHE management systems. Whilst it is concerned mainly with the financial savings arising from a reduction in accidents and the benefits of enhanced project performances, it must always be borne in mind that the provision of a safe working environment is a moral, ethical and legal duty upon the employer. The primary purpose of any SHE management system must always be the avoidance of death and injury at work to persons and the suffering with which this is associated.

Initially the chapter identifies the SHE cost categories. The cost expectations gap is then described followed by a discussion on the cost benefits of SHE management.

As with all management and control there are up-front costs, both at a corporate and project level, associated with the introduction and implementation of SHE management. These highly visible costs are often seen as a barrier to implementation. However, it has been demonstrated that these "costs" are more than offset by the "hidden" benefit of planning and doing things right. The introduction and use of SHE management makes good business and commercial sense and is as much part of the role of management as is the control of quality and productivity.

Having recognised the benefits of SHE management, it is important to understand and identify the associated project SHE costs. These must be acknowledged and, where necessary, priced by those undertaking the construction work. Similarly the benefits of SHE management must accrue to all parties involved in the project. It is only by recognising that the cost benefit equation is heavily biased towards benefit, that successfull proactive management of SHE can be achieved.

6.2   SHE Cost Categories

6.2.1   Costs of Incidents
In the UK the Health and Safety Executive published a guidance document which details typical costs[1]

The costs associated with SHE incidents and accidents can be categorised under the following headings.

- Management and Organisation
  - Management resources
  - Administration
  - Accident investigation

- Damage to reputation
  - Adverse publicity and impact on industrial relations
  - Impact on pre-qualification rating
  - Liability
  - Compensation

- Loss of productivity

- Litigation and Legal Fees

- Delays

- Sick Pay

- Damage to property and materials

- Fines

- Increased insurance premiums

- Medical costs

6.2.2   Costs of Pro-active SHE Management

The "costs" associated with the implementation of SHE management can be categorised under the following headings.

- Establishment of Policy and overall company management systems

- SHE management and organisation for project
  - Supervision
  - Professionals

- Project SHE costs
  - Orientation and training
  - Promotion and publicity
  - Incentive schemes
  - Provision of Personal Protective Equipment
  - Monitoring and inspection
  - Audit and performance measurement
  - Incident/Accident reporting

- Client administrative costs
  - Contract documentation
  - SHE plan
  - On-site monitoring and control

Numerous organisations have demonstrated that the commercial and business benefit of SHE systems far outweigh the initial and ongoing costs.

In addition for the UK the Construction (Design and Management) Regulations 1994 require that the resources allocated to health and safety are adequate. (See Chapter 8).

6.3   SHE Cost Expectation Gap

In setting up systems to manage the SHE aspects, all parties must recognise both the implicit and explicit SHE costs. Where possible, SHE activities should be explicitly included in the tender documentation for pricing by the contractor. These explicit costs are likely to be attributable to specific project activities, eg. the provision of scaffolding or the removal of asbestos during demolition of an old boiler house etc, but can be in the form of a priced SHE specification.

Where project SHE activities, and hence costs, are not explicit in the contractual arrangements, a cost expectation gap is likely to arise during project execution. The cost expectation gap represents the difference between the Client's SHE expectations and the provisions priced by the contractor.

The SHE cost expectation gap can arise due to:

- Over expectations of the client

- Poor communication of exact requirements

- Project specific requirements not recognised by the client.

- Delay in execution of project

To minimise the SHE cost expectation gap, a number of questions should be considered whilst developing bills and schedules for subsequent pricing, including:

- What could cause a cost gap?

- What costs are necessary to close the gap?

Identification of potential cost gaps, together with an analysis of the project requirements will provide the items that should be priced by the contractor.

These items should not include activities and systems which contractors should already have in place as part of their SHE policy and compliance with statutory requirements, nor items that are recognised as good construction practice.

The priced provision of SHE items in bills of quantities will ensure that the contractor has recognised the client's requirements and will acquaint the client with the contractor's commitments.

6.4   Benefits

The fundamental benefit of implementing and using a proactive SHE management system is the reduction of death and injury at work arising from accidents. Following from this is the avoidance of costs that would otherwise be incurred when accidents or incidents occur. Benefits to both parties are achieved through avoidance of:

- Delays to the project

- Damage to plant and equipment

- Involvement in litigation

- Management effort in accident/incident investigations

A large and often unrecognised benefit to both client and contractor comes from enhanced project performance. A safe, tidy site with good access is likely to be an efficient site with:

- High morale

- Fewer disputes

- Reduced absenteeism and labour turnover

- Enhanced teamworking

- Better relationships

High management standards will not be confined to SHE aspects only; project cost, time and quality should all benefit.

_____

1   "The Cost of Accidents at Work". HS (G) 96. ISBN 0 11 886374 6

CHAPTER 7

CONTRACTUAL ARRANGEMENTS

7.1   Introduction

The Contractual arrangements and contract documentation between the various parties involved in a construction project should allocate the rights and obligations of the parties to that contract and the risks to be borne by each party. The contract should also detail the project SHE requirements, obligations and expectations. The contract will provide a framework for defining the required Client, Designer, Planning Supervisor, Principal Contractor and Contractors SHE procedures and control systems.   However contracts do not, and cannot, remove responsibilities imposed under SHE Legislation.

The contractual arrangements will vary greatly depending upon the contract strategy adopted for a particular project. Such strategy will vary from the traditional (employer procures design and contractor builds to that design) to turn-key (contractor undertakes to design and build the project). The contract strategy will also reflect the nature of the project, i.e. whether it is the construction of buildings, civil engineering or process plant erection.

It should also be borne in mind that there will be a number of contracts and again the precise number will depend upon the complexity of the project. Contracts should however exist between:

- Joint venture partners (Client)
- Client - Designer (Engineers/Architects etc)
- Client - Planning Supervisor
- Client - Principal Contractor
- Client - Contractor(s)
- Principal Contractor - Contractor(s) and/or sub-contractors

The above relationships will be affected by the strategy of the contract and will clearly differ between traditional contracts, design and construct contracts and management contracts. Some contractual links may be merged e.g. the Principal Contractor may be appointed as Planning Supervisor.

Consideration of the contract strategy for the project is one of the important project decisions and will determine the criteria for SHE management. The identification and definition of contractual arrangements should be developed with the project SHE plan (see Chapter 5).

The Temporary or Mobile Construction Sites Directive to be implemented by EC countries and implemented in the UK as the Construction (Design and Management) Regulations 1995 sets out clearly obligations and responsibilities as they relate to Client, Designers, Planning Supervisors, Principal Contractors and Contractors. It is essential that any contract strategy should recognise relevant legislation and be consistent with that legislation. This chapter therefore takes due cognisance of that directive because responsibilities imposed by legislation cannot be devolved unto others and the chapter also identifies the major SHE elements to be addressed in contractual arrangements. A check list of items that should be included in the contract documentation has been developed and is set out later in this chapter.

7.2   Pre Contract Considerations

Any contractual implications of SHE issues should be considered prior to drawing up contract documents.

The Client will have to give full consideration to the responsibilities that precede the letting of contracts to the Principal Contractor such as appointing a Designer and Planning Supervisor as well as commencing the SHE Plan.

The Client should also set the criteria which will be used to evaluate tender responses.

To ensure meaningful comparisons can be made between competing bids, the SHE criteria used to evaluate tender responses should be explicitly stated in the tender documentation. In particular these will include:

- The manner of pricing SHE requirements.

- SHE record including any previous prosecution by enforcing authorities.

- Principal Contractor SHE management systems and structures.

- Demonstration of senior management commitment to SHE.

- Specific client requirements.

- Other project specific criteria.

7.3 Contractual Arrangements - Forms of Contract

The contractual implications of SHE issues should be considered prior to drawing up contract documents.

The contract strategy adopted must ensure that the contractor has independent responsibility for complying with the SHE Plan.

7.3.1 Contract Documents

The contract may consist of numerous documents containing typically either one or more or all of the following

- Terms of conditions
- Specification
- Schedules

The form of contract adopted by the client will prescribe the relationships involved in a construction project, it will also determine how much of the project SHE management is relinquished to the Principal Contractor and specifically will set out the responsibilities of each party. Consequently the choice of the form of contract is important as it will influence the management of the SHE matters during the execution of the project.

Issues that should be considered include:

- Form of contract

- Legislation and Codes of Practice

- SHE expectations and requirements

- Principal Contractor resources

- Recognition and management of interfaces

- The criteria that will be used to evaluate tender response

The following is an example of possible contractual relationships under what might be termed the "traditional" contractual arrangement, i.e. an employer who uses a professional designer to design a project to be constructed by a Principal Contractor. The duties listed are those that might typically flow from the directive but these will vary from country to country depending upon how the directive has been implemented. UK terminology and duties are referred to in this example.

7.3.2 Typical Contractual Arrangement

Client - Designer

- provide all necessary information
- make available the SHE File (if any)
- appoint a competent Planning Supervisor
- commence a SHE plan
- appoint a competent Principal Contractor

- liaise with Planning Supervisor
- ensure design considerations include
  - avoidance of foreseeable risks
  - combating risks at source
  - measures of protection
  - provision of adequate information
- liaise with Principal Contractor

Client - Planning Supervisor

Client Obligations

- appoint competent Designer
- ensure SHE File available (if any)
- provide necessary information
- provide an initial SHE plan
- appoint competent Principal Contractor and

Planning Supervisor Obligations

- development of SHE plan by due date
- ensure as far as reasonably practical that design includes adequate regard to avoidance of foreseeable risks, combating of risks at source, measures of protection and the provision of adequate information
- give notice to HSE
- provision of SHE file

Client - Principal Contractor

- appoint competent Designer and Planning Supervisor
- ensure production of SHE plan prior to construction

- develop the SHE plan and file
- ensure co-operation between contractors
- ensure compliance with rules in the SHE plan
- allow only authorised persons onto site
- provide Planning Supervisor with information
- ensure contractors received information on risks
- ensure employees and self-employed can discuss safety and health

Client - Contractor

Client Obligations	Contractor Obligations
- appoint competent Designer, Planning Supervisor and Principal Contractor - ensure SHE file and plan made available - ensure necessary information made available	- co-operate with Principal Contractor - provide Principal Contractor with information - comply with rules in SHE plan and Principal Contractor requirements - provide accident information to Principal Contractor - provide information to Principal Contractor that Planning Supervisor requires

It should be emphasised that there are many contractual methods of procurement but it is suggested that the above sets out the main contractual obligations required by the UK's CDM regulations.

Other matters that should be incorporated into the contractual framework are set out below.

- In particular the requirement of the Directive as enacted in a particular country should be established as well as legislation applicable to a particular aspect of the project, e.g. demolition, asbestos etc.

7.3.3   Standard Contracts

There are of course many standard contracts in use which deal with different relationships (e.g. Client's contracts with consultants and Client's contracts with Contractors). It is clear that standard contracts will require amendments most notably those contracts dealing with the relationship between Client and professional consultants (e.g. engineers, architects etc), and there will probably be standard contracts for then Client Planning Supervisor relationship.

Certain of the standard contracts will or have been altered to reflect the new requirements and users of those contracts should refer to the relevant body.

7.3.4   SHE Expectations and Requirements

Each contract must include a brief but comprehensive description of the work and SHE related issues, identifying the following items.

- General scope
- Appointment and role of Planning Supervisor
- Framework and procedures to deal with SHE file and SHE plan
- Specific Hazards such as:
  - Asbestos
  - Excavations
  - Demolition etc.
  - Falls and working at height
  - Falling materials
  - Transport
- Role of Designer and liaison with Designer
- Implications of schedule on SHE management
- SHE controls, monitoring, audits and inspection

Project organisation and interfaces must be determined to ensure that responsibilities are recognised and correctly assigned within the contract framework. Including SHE issues relating to:

- Use of sub-contractors
- Suppliers - Supply and use of hazardous materials
- Design
- Management of sub-contractor's and suppliers' SHE policy

7.3.5 Principal Contractor and Contractor Resources

The contractual arrangements should explicitly identify the Principal Contractor and contractor resources necessary to meet the SHE requirements of the project.

- Management and organisation
  - Company organisation
  - Project organisation
  - Professional expertise

- Skill base
  - Specific experience in operations such as demolition

- Specific project training requirements
  - Does the project team require specific SHE training?

- Schedule requirements
  - The contractor's programme should recognise the implications of complying with project SHE requirements and procedures.

- Define the project controls and the requirements for monitoring and auditing.

- Detail enforcement and remedies for non-compliance with SHE plan.

- Identify SHE issues relevant to specific project activities, such as:
  - Lifting operations
  - Demolition
  - Hazardous materials

- Identify specific SHE skills and training requirements

- Detail procedures for accident investigation, report and follow-up

- Make provision for client enforcement action of SHE requirements.

7.4 Check List

To aid preparation of the contractual arrangements, the following checklist has been developed. The checklist is not exhaustive and particular attention should be paid to project specific SHE issues.

7.4.1 Management and Leadership

- Principal Contractor acknowledges at director level the Client's strong commitment to health and safety and is committed to achieve the requirements of the SHE specification included within the contract documents.

- Client acknowledges at director level the Client's obligations to health and safety, and has produced a SHE specification.

- Client confirms the Designer is similarly committed to the SHE policy.

- Client has appointed a Planning Supervisor to assist in the production of SHE file and SHE plan.

- Client shall make available all necessary information.

- Principal Contractor confirms that its SHE policy and operational procedures are of a standard not less than those required by the Client.

- Principal Contractor confirms that the same standard will be required of sub-contractors.

- Principal Contractor confirms that the SHE policy is widely disseminated.

- Principal Contractor advises on the arrangements to vet contractors and/or sub-contractors. This could be achieved by using the Client's selection procedures.

- Principal Contractor confirms:

  - Understanding of the Client's standards, applicable health and safety law, knowledge of substances used on site and any other hazards unique to the project.

  - Support of the Client's Planning Supervisor, SHE file, SHE plan and safety incentive schemes, surveys etc.

  - Understanding that any infringements of law, regulations or safe operating standards are to be remedied by the contractor.

  - Understanding of the Client's right to stop work until any unsafe act or situation has been rectified.

  - Understanding that repeated infringement of SHE requirement could lead to:

    Replacement of staff on the project
    Termination of Contract
    Removal from approved bidders list.

  - That appropriate funds have been made available to comply with all aspects of the SHE Specification. (Certain clients require SHE costings to be identified in a separate specification).

7.4.2   Organisation and Rules

- All Contractors are required to define their SHE organisation for the project.

- The SHE organisation must identify clearly the line management responsibility for SHE at each level in the Contractor's organisation.

- The SHE organisation must identify clearly the line management responsibility for SHE at each level in the Contractor's organisation.

- The Principal Contractor must notify the Client of the name of the nominated person responsible for safety.

- The Principal Contractor must only provide staff who are suitably trained, competent and qualified for the SHE tasks they are to perform whether they are line management or members of the SHE organisation.

- The SHE specification provides the Client with the right to inspect the training, competence and qualifications of personnel with responsibilities under the SHE organisation.

- The Principal Contractor shall comply with all applicable SHE rules for working on the Client's project. These should be incorporated in the contract documents by the Client.

- The Principal Contractor shall require the workforce to comply with these SHE rules and include them in the terms and conditions of employment issued to the workforce.

7.4.3   SHE Training

- Principal Contractor shall ensure that all personnel and those of sub-contractors are adequately trained in the SHE requirements of the Client. The Contractor's personnel shall be competent to undertake the work and fully trained in the tasks to be performed.

- Principal Contractor must specify requirements regarding induction in SHE matters.

- Client's right to attend Principal Contractor induction and other SHE management and employee training sessions.

- The Principal Contractor must provide adequate SHE training regarding employees' responsibilities and identify specific SHE training programme appropriate to the Contract.

- Principal Contractor should make available all records of training.

7.4.4   Control of on-site design changes

- Ensure site based modifications receive appropriate approval from the designers.

7.4.5   Working Procedures

- Construction tasks involving high or known risks should be listed in the SHE plan, e.g.
  - Demolition
  - Steel erection
  - Roofing works.

- Work method statements must be produced for all hazardous operations to be carried out by the Principal Contractor, prior to commencement of the task, whether or not they were identified in the SHE specification.

- The Principal Contractor shall describe the sequence of erection and proposed construction methods, supported by diagrams and drawings, showing the movement of materials and plant onto the site and into their final position. The Method Statement shall also cover safety arrangements for personnel, for example, means of access.

- The SHE specification should require the Principal Contractor to advise the name of the individual appointed as safety supervisor/adviser.

- Principal Contractor shall continually update and develop the SHE file originally provided by the Client Planning Supervisor and develop as necessary the SHE plan.

7.4.6 Procurement Controls

The party responsible for procurement or purchasing should:

- Ensure compliance with National Standards, Codes, inspection, testing, verification.

- Ensure compliance with relevant SHE legislation.

- Ensure that the safest materials are chosen from the possible alternatives.

- Ensure full SHE documentation is received relevant to the control of substances hazardous to health and any necessary actions taken to control risks to employees and others.

7.4.7 Emergency Procedures

- SHE specification requires Principal Contractor to comply with Client emergency procedures.

- The Principal Contractor must ensure employees are fully trained in the emergency procedures.

- The Principal Contractor accepts the Client's right to inspect Principal Contractor's emergency arrangements and training provisions.

- The Principal Contractor and Client should agree how all necessary emergency equipment, within his area of control e.g. first aid, fire extinguishers, protective equipment, is to be provided and serviced.

7.4.8 Planned Inspections

- SHE specification shall require Principal Contractors and their sub-contractors to undertake their own programme of SHE inspections and to advise the Client of the results.

- SHE specification shall allow Client access to inspect any plant, equipment, personnel and related records relevant to health and safety and the work environment.

- SHE specification shall require the Principal Contractor to rectify promptly any deficiencies observed during any inspection, and to notify the client of the results of any inspections by the enforcing authorities.

7.4.9   SHE Audits

- The Principal Contractor should be required to provide a system of formal SHE auditing covering all aspects of site operations.

- The Principal Contractor should be required to demonstrate that the results of the SHE audit are fed back through all levels of the organisation.

7.4.10   Incident/Accident Investigations

- The SHE specification requires the Principal Contractor to have an incident/accident reporting system which is compatible with legislative and Client's requirements, which will cover all accidents and incidents including those affecting the public.

- The Principal Contractor is required to advise the Client immediately of any reportable injury, major injury, fatality or dangerous occurrence.

- The Principal Contractor is required to provide competent and well trained staff with clearly defined responsibilities for accident/incident reporting.

- The Principal Contractor is required to provide an analysis of all accidents and incidents. This will include:
  - Minor injuries
  - Reportable injuries
  - Major injuries
  - Fatalities
  - Dangerous occurrences
  - Accident frequency rate
  - Accident type/incident rate
  - Injury type
  - Causation
  - Fires

- All incident/accident data to be presented in a format previously agreed with the Client.

- Incident/accident data should be analysed on a regular basis. Trends in incidents/accidents should be communicated to all interested parties with appropriate recommendations.

7.4.11   Recruitment and Placement

- Principal Contractor confirms that the recruitment and placement processes take into account the need for all personnel engaged in work on site to be suitably competent, trained and to possess the necessary physical and intellectual qualities required for the job.

- Principal Contractor confirms that SHE factors are duly considered in recruitment and selection criteria.

- Principal Contractor confirms that SHE factors have suitable prominence in assessing employees' performance and suitability for career development.

- Principal Contractor confirms that terms and conditions of employment cover SHE requirements. Employees are informed of these requirements by written notification and induction.

- Principal Contractor confirms that any specific training needs are identified at hiring such as:
  - Abrasive wheels
  - Forklift truck driving.

7.4.12   Occupational Health

- Principal Contractor shall ensure that all employees are medically fit for the work to be done. An employee with any disabilities must be reported to the Client prior to work starting, and arrangements for their safety, especially in emergency situations confirmed.

- Principal Contractor is required to provide a safe and healthy workplace for his employees.

- Principal Contractor is required to provide information on any substances that may pose a health hazard to his employees (COSHH), and others working in close proximity, where the use of such substances cannot be avoided.

- Principal Contractor is required to review construction work practices for the site in order to remove or reduce hazardous operations.

7.4.13   Personal Protective Equipment (PPE)

- SHE specification requires the Principal Contractor to supply, at his own expense, any protective equipment both personal and task issue.

- SHE specification requires the Principal Contractor to provide adequate and secure provision for storage of PPE when not in use and procedure for ensuring adequacy of stock.

- SHE specification requires Principal Contractor to ensure as far as practicable that employees wear the PPE issued to them on all relevant occasions.

- Principal Contractor undertakes to co-operate with Client regarding the compliance of the workforce on the wearing of PPE and the maintenance of suitable records.

7.4.14   Communications

- Principal Contractor to confirm arrangements for personal communication from senior management through supervision to the workforce.

- Principal Contractor to undertake that (as a minimum) the following activities take place:
  - Supervisors/workforce - regular tool box talks
  - Supervisors/new starts - induction training
  - Management meeting with Supervision and Safety Representatives.

7.4.15 Meetings

- Principal Contractor confirms that regular group meetings will take place to review SHE matters.

- Principal Contractor to provide programme of meetings, agenda and minutes to Client.

- Client to specify requirements for Principal Contractor to participate, with Client and other parties, in regular site SHE meetings. Parties involved may include:
  - Client
  - Planning Supervisor
  - Contractor
  - Sub-contractor
  - Safety Adviser
  - Appointed Safety Representatives.

7.4.16 Promotions

- Principal Contractor confirms willingness to participate in project SHE promotions and initiatives, e.g.
  - SHE motivation programmes
  - SHE safety surveys.

- Principal Contractor confirms due allowance has been made within the tender to participate in Project SHE initiatives, e.g.
  - Poster campaigns
  - Competitions
  - Notice boards
  - Induction courses
  - Suggestion schemes.

7.4.17 Off the Job Safety

- Principal Contractor confirms that off the job safety will be promoted through an established SHE programme.

CHAPTER 8

ASSESSMENT OF COMPETENCE AND RESOURCES

8.1   Introduction

The Client has an absolute duty to ensure that designers, planning supervisors, principal contractors and contractors are competent;

•   To perform any requirement and

•   To conduct their undertaking without contravening any prohibition imposed by statute.

In addition the client has to ascertain

•   what resources have been or are intended to be allocated and

•   whether those resources are adequate.

Where any of the roles are carried out by the client's employees it is necessary to clearly assign the responsibilities identified and ensure that staff have sufficient time and, where necessary, resources to carry out the duties allocated to them and as identified from the SHE Plan for the project.

i.e.   Identify key staff

Allocate such staff

Determine competence

Train staff as necessary

Where any of the duties or roles are carried out by external organisations, such as consultants, contractors or agency staff then reasonable enquiries must be carried out to determine competence and adequate resources. The enquiries should be appropriate to the amount of work, and the known risks.

In checking on competence, those making the checks should take account of the need for:

•   A knowledge and understanding of the work involved, the management and prevention of risk and of relevant SHE standards; and

•   The capacity to apply this knowledge and experience to the work required in relation to the particular project for which the Planning Supervisor, designer or Principal Contractor is being engaged.

8.1.1   The Planning Supervisor

In making enquiries when appointing the Planning Supervisor, the client should check that the Planning Supervisor has the necessary knowledge and ability to fulfil the responsibilities of the role.

The reasonable steps to be taken may include checking:

- the Planning Supervisor's knowledge of construction practice, particularly in relation to the nature of the project;

- familiarity and knowledge of the design function;

- knowledge of SHE issues, particularly in preparing a SHE plan;

- ability to work with and co-ordinate the activities of different designers and be a bridge between the design function sand construction work on site;

- the number, experience and qualification of people to be employed, both internally and from other sources, to perform the various functions in relation to the project;

- the management systems which will be used to monitor the correct allocation of people and other resources in the way agreed at the time when these matters are being finalised;

- the time to be allowed to carry out the different duties; and

- the technical facilities available to aid the staff in carrying out their duties.

8.1.2   Designers

Anyone who engages a designer should check the knowledge, ability and resources of the designer to carry out the duties and provide advice. In carrying out checks, those who engage designers may wish to seek advice where necessary.

The reasonable steps to be taken may include enquiries as to:

- familiarity with construction processes in the circumstances of the project and the impact of design on SHE;

- awareness of relevant SHE legislation and appropriate risk assessment methods;

- the people to be employed to carry out the work, their skills and training; this will include external resources where necessary, and review of the design against the requirements of the client or legislation (CF CDM Regulation 13);

- the time allowed to fulfil the various elements of the designer's work;

- the technical facilities available to support the designer, particularly in the circumstances of the project;

- the method of communicating design decisions to ensure that the resources to be allocated are clear, and,

- the way in which information will be communicated on the remaining risks, after the statutory duties (CDM regulation 13 (a)) have been complied with .

8.1.3   The Principal Contractor

In making enquiries about the Principal Contractor, the client should check the Principal Contractor's knowledge, ability and resources to carry out the duties of the role.

The competence of and the resources which will be allocated by the Principal Contractor have to be judged against how the construction phase will be managed so as to implement the SHE plan. The content of the plan may influence the extent of the checks. The checks made about contractors are also relevant to those made of the Principal Contractor. In making decisions, those who engage the Principal Contractor can seek advice where necessary, including from the Planning Supervisor.

The reasonable steps to be taken may include enquiries as to:

* the people to carry out or manage the work, their skills, knowledge, experience and training;

* the time allowed to complete various stages of the construction work without risks to health and safety;

* the way people are to be employed to ensure compliance with SHE legislation;

* the technical and managerial approach for dealing with the risks specified in the SHE plan.

8.2   Assessment of Competence and Resources

Contractors may be employed to act not only during the construction phase of a project but also during the design and planning phases (Refer Chapter 7). It is essential that the client takes steps to ensure that those employed are competent to perform their allocated duties.

The objective of this section is to provide a framework which can be used to evaluate the competence of potential contractors at both the pre qualification and tender evaluation stages of a contract. Whilst recognising that these two stages are complementary, the requirements of each are different. The information should be analysed in a way which allows the person evaluating the bids to compare different contractors on a 'like for like' basis.

8.2.1   Summary of Key Issues

The primary purpose of assessment procedures are to achieve:

* Confirmation that the tenderer has recognised the SHE requirements and expectations of the project.

* A thorough evaluation of each tenderer's SHE plans to ensure they achieve at least the minimum acceptable standards defined in the contract documentation.

* An evaluation and comparison of the SHE aspects in competing bids.

* A checklist of SHE items to be clarified by the tenderer.

* The inclusion of suitable cost provisions for SHE activities.

Assessment consists of two phases:

* Pre-qualification

* Tender Evaluation

8.2.2   Pre-qualification

Screening of potential tenderer's to confirm that they have the necessary expertise, experience and capability to undertake the required role.

Screening arrangements should include
- Questionnaire
- Evaluation of previous experience of potential tenderer
- Assessment of potential tenderer general reputation within industry.
- SHE Policy evaluation

8.2.3   Tender Evaluation

Evaluate and compare SHE aspects of bid responses

- SHE plans

- Key personnel

- Proposed sub-contractors

- Management / Method statements for project specific SHE issues

- Provision of costs for SHE activities

- Provision of SHE training

8.3   Pre qualification Stage

Screening of potential tenderer's to confirm that they have the necessary expertise, experience and capability to undertake the project.

Used to prepare a list of potential tenderers who may be invited to bid for a project.

Should identify those who are clearly unsuitable to undertake the work by identifying deficiencies in their organisation and administration arrangements which would suggest that they would be unable to undertake the SHE requirements of the project.

May be used for a one off project or to provide a pool of tenderers who may be invited to submit bids for a series of projects (i.e. may need to be updated from time to time).

Screening arrangements should include:

- Questionnaire

- Evaluation of previous experience of tenderer

- Assessment of tenderer's general reputation within industry.

- Examination of SHE Policy

- Provision of specific services

Review selection criteria against current project plan to ensure that assumptions used to define criteria are still valid.

Checklist

To aid development of an assessment strategy the following checklist has been developed. The checklist is not exhaustive and particular attention should be paid to project specific SHE issues.

8.3.1   Management And Leadership

- Assess commitment and attitude to project SHE objectives.

- Review SHE performance on previous projects (where possible)
  - SHE problems on other sites

- Review proposed management team's SHE experience
  - CVs etc.

- Seek evidence that SHE objectives are given the appropriate priority compared with other management objectives, including :
  - General objectives
  - Project specific objectives
  - Training.

- Review quality of relationships with external SHE authorities.

8.3.2   Organisations and Rules

- Review organisational structure with specific reference to:
  - Company organisation for general SHE including director responsible for SHE
  - Company organisation for project SHE
  - Line responsibility for SHE

- Review actual rules issued to employees

- Review SHE consultation structures

- How is compliance with SHE rules reviewed/enforced ?

- Is the need for specific SHE rules for each project reviewed ?

- Are external SHE advisers employed ?
  - On what basis?
  - Input into project SHE

- Do job descriptions and personnel specifications define SHE responsibilities?

- Review training, competence and experience of SHE specialist and advisers

- Location and use of SHE policy documentation and manuals

8.3.3   SHE Training

- Assess the adequacy of training provided to all levels in the organisation

- Review contents of induction courses:
  - Policy, organisation and arrangements
  - Definition of responsibilities
  - Safe systems of work
  - Targets and performance criteria.

- Review content of internal and external training courses used

- Is special training provided in areas such as:
  - Operation of plant and machinery?
  - First Aid?

- Review ongoing and on the job training procedures

- Training in emergency procedures

8.3.4   Control of on-site design changes

- Assess the adequacy of procedures for design change controls

8.3.5   Working Procedures

- Do working procedures ensure that SHE objectives are met?

- Are project SHE hazards systematically assessed ?

- Provision of written method statements

- Provision and use of safe working systems such as:
  - Heavy lifting procedure
  - Permit to work procedures
  - Excavations
  - Working at height
  - Use and handling of Radioactive sources
  - Demolition
  - Steel erection
  - Lasers
  - Handling and use of hazardous substances.

- Procedures to advise statutory and regulatory authorities of "high risk" activities.

8.3.6   Procurement Controls

- How is it ensured that the project SHE requirements are imposed on vendors? e.g:

  - Provision of SHE information with new equipment

  - Written specifications for key items

- Provision of data relating to chemical composition and hazards of substances purchased.

- Inspection of items when received

- Handling, storage and control of received items.

8.3.7   Emergency Procedures

- Assess the emergency procedures
  - General competence of personnel
  - Understanding of required actions

- Assess the procedures for dealing with emergency situations such as:
  - Excavation collapse
  - Localised fires
  - Means of escape
  - Site evacuation
  - Toxic gas escape
  - Fire / explosions.

- What emergency first aid facilities are provided ?

8.3.8   Planned Inspections

- What arrangements/procedures are in place for SHE inspection and audit, including corrective actions?

- Review the arrangements to comply with statutory requirements for inspection, examination and notification of items such as:
  - Cranes, plant and equipment
  - Excavations
  - Scaffolds.

- Review "house keeping" arrangements

8.3.9   SHE Audits

- Is a formal auditing system used?

- What are the details of the auditing system?

- How are the results of audits fed back and disseminated throughout the organisation?

8.3.10   Incident/Accident Investigations

- What systems are in place for Incident / Accident investigation and reporting?

- Who has responsibility for such investigations?

- What are their competencies and have they been trained?

- How are the results from investigations communicated and followed up throughout the organisation?
  - Amendments to procedures
  - Implementation of recommendations

- Are incident and accident statistics kept ? Such as:
  - Accident frequency rates
  - Prohibition, improvement notices and prosecutions
  - Fatalities
  - Lost time due to injuries
  - Property damage and near misses.

- How long are these statistics kept for?

- How are the statistics used?
  - Formulation of SHE policy?
  - In forming SHE action plans?

8.3.11   Recruitment and Placement

- Review procedures for hiring and placement:
  - Are SHE factors used in selection criteria?
  - Are SHE factors used in employee performance appraisal?

- When evidence of lack of SHE competence exists, what actions are taken?

- Is it ensured that adequate record keeping, certification, etc, is monitored for staff undertaking specialised trades.

8.3.12   Occupational Health

- What arrangements are in place to provide a healthy workplace for its employees?

- What instruction/information is provided to employees on occupational health hazards?

- Are employees required to undertake regular medical examinations?

- Are medical examinations a part of the recruitment process?

- Are reviews of work practices carried out with a view to eliminating or reducing hazardous working conditions?

- What are the procedures for assessing project health risks prior to project execution?

8.3.13   Personal Protective Equipment (PPE)

- Is there proof that PPE is only provided as a last resort ?
- How is personal protective equipment used ?
  - Inventory management
  - Provision of PPE to employees
  - Instruction in use
  - Records of issue and training
  - Cleaning, maintenance and storage

- Do project planning procedures recognise the provision of personal protective equipment?

8.3.14 Communications

- How are SHE requirements and expectations communicated to employees and their representatives
  - Formal issue
  - Notice boards
  - Safety bulletins etc
  - Via supervisors (toolbox talks etc)

- Do senior management communicate a commitment to SHE by their actions for example by visiting and walking the site?

- What role do SHE professionals have in communicating SHE issues?

8.3.15 Meetings

- Are regular meetings on SHE matters held ?
  - Types of meeting
  - Frequency of meetings
  - Attendance
    - Senior Management
    - Safety committee
    - Safety representatives
    - Employees (Tool box talks)
  - Content
  - Records and minutes

8.3.16 Promotions

- How is acceptable SHE behaviour promoted ?
  - Posters
  - Notice boards
  - Videos etc

- Is there a willingness to be involved in site-wide co-ordination of SHE initiatives?

- What experience is there in SHE motivational schemes?

- How are SHE suggestions from employees dealt with ?

8.3.17 Off the Job Safety

- What action does is taken to promote SHE issues outside the workplace?

8.4 Tender assessment/evaluation stage

Screening of tenderer's to determine that they have the necessary competence i.e. skills and expertise to carry out the project in accordance with the SHE plan.

Confirmation that they have allocated sufficient resources and allowed sufficient time to complete the project in accordance with the project SHE plan.

Evaluate and compare SHE aspects of bid responses

- SHE plan

- Key personnel

- Proposed Sub contractors

- Method statements for specific SHE issues

- Provision of resources for SHE activities

- Provision of SHE training

- Monitoring of activities

Checklist

To aid development of a strategy for assessing the SHE aspects of bids the following checklist has been developed. The checklist is not exhaustive and particular attention should be paid to project specific SHE issues.

8.4.1   SHE plan

- Assess the procedures which will be adopted for developing and implementing the SHE plan

- Determine whether the risks identified in the plan, have been adequately addressed and sufficient steps taken to control them.

- Determine whether all the hazards arising from the operations have been identified and sufficient steps taken to control them.

- Assess the time allowed to complete the various stages of the project without risks to SHE.

8.4.2   Management Systems

- The arrangements to be put in place to actively manage SHE.

    - Project specific policy

    - Provision of and access to specialist advice

    - Quality plans and programme

    - Audits and survelliance

- Review proposed management teams SHE experience - CV's etc.

8.4.3   Co-operation with and co-ordination of contractors activities

- What arrangements will be in place to ensure that project activities do not create a hazard to other employees and vice versa.

- How will the SHE performance of contractors be assessed?

8.4.4 Involvement of employees

- How will SHE information be provided to employees?

- What arrangement will be made to seek the views of employees on SHE matters ?

- What training will be provided to employees?

8.4.5 Compliance with statutory requirements

- How will statutory requirements be complied with e.g.

  - Assessments of risk such as chemicals or noise

  - Accident reporting and investigation procedures.

  - Provision and use of personal protective equipment.

  - Welfare arrangements

8.4.6 Specific SHE initiatives

- Planned inspections

- Toolbox talks

- Safety promotions

- Safety Awareness campaigns

WORKED EXAMPLE 8.1

CONTRACTOR SHE PRE-QUALIFICATION

Questionnaires should include information required to assess the extent of SHE management systems and procedures used by the contractor.

Emphasis should be placed on the need for complete answers substantiated by supporting documentation as far as is practicable.

Submissions should be assessed using an explicit scoring mechanism.

The following details suitable questions that could be asked of a potential contractor.

SHE ASSESSMENT QUESTIONNAIRE

1. **She Policy, Organisation and Management Involvement**

1.1   Do you have a SHE Policy?   Y/N

     Is this signed by the senior executive?   Y/N

     Please supply a copy

1.2   Does a SHE structure exist in your organisation?   Y/N

     Please provide details

1.3   Are senior and middle management actively involved in the promotion

     of SHE ?   Y/N

     Please provide details e.g.

     Periodical work area inspections

     Regular SHE meetings with personnel

1.4   Are the SHE responsibilities of managers clearly defined ?   Y/N

     Please provide details

1.5   Are annual SHE objectives included in your business plan ?   Y/N

     Please provide examples

2. **SHE Training**

2.1   Is training provided to employees at the following stages?

     •   When joining the company   Y/N

     •   When changing jobs within the company   Y/N

     •   When new plant or equipment needs to be operated   Y/N

     •   As a result of experience of and feedback from accident/incident

          reports   Y/N

     Are you able to provide proof of specialist training provided?   Y/N

     Please state how this can be achieved.

2.2   What formal SHE training is provided specifically to

     •   First line supervisors?

     •   Middle and top level management?

     Please describe

2.3 Are all employees (including subcontractors) instructed as to the application

of rules and regulations ? Y/N

When is this done and how it is achieved ?

2.4 Does this training include the selection, use and care of personal

protective equipment ? Y/N

2.5 What SHE refresher training is provided and at what intervals ?

Please list examples

Course title	Target audience	Interval

2.6 Has the person(s) allocated as your SHE adviser followed

specific SHE training ? Y/N

Please list most recent courses

Does this include refresher training ? Y/N

3. Purchase of Goods, Materials and Services

3.1 Do you have a system for establishing SHE specification

as part of the assessment of goods, materials and services ? Y/N

Please describe

3.2 Do you have a system which ensures that all statutory inspections

of plant and equipment are carried out ? Y/N

Please give examples of plant/equipment covered

3.3 Is there a record of inspections ? Y/N

Where is this kept ?

3.4 How is plant and equipment which has been inspected identified as being

safe to use ?

3.5 Do you evaluate the SHE competence of all sub contractors ? Y/N

Please describe how this is achieved and how the results are monitored.

4. SHE Inspections

4.1 Are periodic work inspections carried out by first line supervisors ? Y/N

4.2	Are records of these inspections kept available ?	Y/N
4.3	During the inspections are supervisors required to check that safety rules and regulations (including personal protective equipment) are adhered to ?	Y/N
4.4	Are unsafe acts and conditions reported and remedial actions formally monitored ?	Y/N

Please provide examples of the above.

5. Rules and Regulations

5.1	Do health and safety rules and regulations exist for personnel and subcontractors ?	Y/N

Do these cover

	General rules	Y/N
	Project rules	Y/N
	Specific task rules	Y/N
5.2	Do these rules include a permit to work system (as applicable)	Y/N
5.3	Do you have experience of project SHE plans as required by legislation ?	Y/N

Please give examples of where these have been used.

5.4	Do you have a formal company guideline for holding pre contract health and safety meetings with the client ?	Y/N

6. Risk Management

6.1 Have the following, involved in the execution of your work, been identified ?

6.1.1	Hazards affecting health and safety	Y/N
6.1.2	The groups of people who might be affected	Y/N
6.1.3	An evaluation of the risk from each significant hazard	Y/N
6.1.4	Whether the risks arising are adequately controlled	Y/N
6.2	Are these findings and assessments recorded	Y/N
6.3	How often are they reviewed	-------- years
6.4	For what processes/risk is personal protective equipment issued	

Process/Risk   Type of PPE

7. **Emergency Arrangements**

7.1 How do you manage your arrangements for dealing with emergencies?

Are these communicated to your sub-contractors? Y/N

7.2 What provision have you made for first aid?

e.g. Trained First Aiders

7.3 What training do you provide to employees in Fire Safety/Fire Fighting ?

8. **Recruitment Personnel**

8.1 Are health and safety factors considered when hiring personnel? Y/N

8.2 Are staff medically examined before hiring?

In all cases Y/N

Where required for

occupational reasons e.g.

Fork Lift Truck Driver Y/N

8.3 How do you assess the competence of staff before appointment ?

(e.g. trade testing, taking up references).

9. **Reporting and Investigation of Accidents, Incidents and Dangerous Conditions**

9.1 Do you have a procedure for reporting, investigating and recording

accidents and incidents? Y/N

Please send a copy

9.2 Is there a standard report/investigation form used? Y/N

Please send a copy

9.3 Do you have a formal system for reporting hazardous situations/near

misses etc ? Y/N

9.4   Please provide the following statistics for the last five years.

	Year 1	Year 2	Year 3	Year 4	Year 5
Lost Time accidents per 100 employees					
Major/Reportable injuries per 100 employees					
Number of Dangerous Occurrences					
Mandays lost due to accidents					

10.   Health and Safety Communication and Consultation

10.1   Are SHE committee meetings held between management and

employees representatives?   Y/N

10.2   Are the results of these meetings communicated to all employees?   Y/N

If yes please describe how

10.3   Are SHE tool box talks held?   Y/N

At what frequency

Led by whom

10.4   Do you carry out SHE promotions/campaigns?   Y/N

Please give examples

CHAPTER 9

PRE-CONSTRUCTION AND CONSTRUCTION PLANNING

9.1   Introduction

Planning should be a continuous process throughout the life of a project, starting with a broad brush approach when the initial concept is being considered and developing as the level of information detail increases. It is essential for success that each stage incorporates and builds on the decisions taken during the previous stages.

The results of this planning must be written down as the SHE plan. The Planning Supervisor appointed by the client must ensure that every designer identifies all significant health and safety issues relevant to his part of the design and incorporates these in a plan. Examples of such issues will be the specifying of materials or substances with health or safety risks to handlers and users, and the resulting precautions which must be taken.

The Planning Supervisor will need to liaise with the client to ensure that information about the state or condition of the premises where the project is to be carried out is obtained and incorporated in the plan. This will include such matters as contaminated ground and suspect existing insulation material.

The client and designers of packages of the project must co-operate with the Planning Supervisor in the provision of SHE information which could be relevant to the wellbeing of persons who are subsequently involved in construction, commissioning, repairing or maintaining the plant. The Planning Supervisor must ensure, in turn that this information is passed on to those persons via the plan.

Whereas the pre-construction planning is the responsibility of the Planning Supervisor, the construction planning is the responsibility of the Principal Contractor appointed by the client. It is the Principal Contractor who develops the SHE plan and ensures it includes the arrangements for the management of the construction work and for monitoring compliance with all relevant requirements.

The Principal Contractor must receive, assess and co-ordinate the safe working methods proposed by the project contractors after they have carried out their risk assessments. The SHE plan must be updated as necessary by the Principal Contractor to incorporate these proposed working methods.

The client should not forget that he has a statutory duty to ensure that no construction work is commenced in the project before the SHE plan is compiled, but this does not mean that it cannot be changed thereafter. Indeed that nature of construction work is such that changes will invariably be necessary. What it does mean however is that the plan must be in sufficient detail prior to construction to cover that part of the construction work which is to be immediately carried out. On most large projects the Planning Supervisor's and Principal Contractor's roles will overlap and they will jointly develop and expand the SHE plan as the design details become further available and contractors proposed working methods received.

Chapter 3 gives guidance in SHE issues which the Planning Supervisor will need to consider when the SHE plan is first being drafted. It will be to the projects considerable advantage, from the point of view of SHE planning, if the Principal Contractor can be appointed as early as possible so that both the Planning Supervisor and the Principal Contractor can jointly develop the project SHE plan. If this is not possible then the Planning Supervisor should obtain additional construction advice.

9.2   Key Issues

The Planning Supervisor and the Principal Contractor should, jointly if possible, consider the following non exhaustive list of issues for inclusion in the SHE plan.

9.2.1   Organisational and Procedural

- The project SHE objectives

- The proposed safety management system including the organisation and arrangements

- The joint and several responsibilities of all the parties

- The identification of and information on significant hazardous operations and materials

- Assessment of risks arising from the identified hazards

- Proposed safe working methods resulting from the risk assessments

- Vendor and contractor prequalification and selection procedures

- Procedures for monitoring compliance with legal requirements and health and safety plan rules

- Auditing arrangements

- Fire precautions

- Emergency and evacuation procedures

- SHE induction and training

- Welfare and medical provisions

- Workforce consultation

- SHE propaganda and incentive schemes

- Security and surveillance

- Clients rules, including permits to work

- Management safety meetings

9.2.2 Site Rules

- Speed limits and parking restrictions
- Authorised entry
- Authorised use and operations of plant and equipment
- Personal protective equipment
- Restricted access areas
- Smoking restrictions/hot work
- Cranage and lifting operations
- Temporary works
- Inspections and examinations
- Scaffolding and access
- Common user services
- Laydown and storage areas
- Tidiness and housekeeping
- Accident and incident reporting and investigation
- Task talks covering risks assessments
- Generic tool box talks
- Noise limitations
- COSHH assessment communication and information exchange
- Confined space entry requirements
- Waste disposal
- Site radiography
- Hydrostatic and pneumatic testing
- Substance screening
- Disciplinary procedures
- Hazardous substances

9.3 Check Lists

9.3.1 Management and Leadership (Client, Planning Supervisor, Principal Contractor)

- Set out managerial responsibilities in the SHE plan and ensure that responsibilities and interfaces are clear between client, Planning Supervisor, Principal Contractor and contractors, covering both temporary and permanent works, including any changes that may occur during the course of the project.

- Ensure that all levels of management maintain high profiles during the planning activities and that the plans produced incorporate the actions necessary to deliver the project's SHE policies, and objectives stated in the SHE plan.

- Appoint project planners with SHE knowledge that includes the construction stage, who are capable of planning SHE considerations into the programme.

- Appoint SHE officers/advisers, with clear objectives, who are accountable to the senior manager.

- Make specialist SHE and technical expertise readily available to the planners and construction staff.

- Ensure that all training covers SHE aspects, including safety, emergency, fire, specialist tasks.

- Ensure that hazards are identified and risks assessed. Where hazards are high ensure that the SHE considerations are recorded and job method statements are developed and made available to the construction teams.

- Allow time in the programme to enable the work to be done safely, including time for the re-evaluation of risks at appropriate stages.

- Set up arrangements to deal with emergencies e.g.: fire, bomb warnings, high winds, power failures.

- Plan to monitor frequency, thoroughness and results of inspections and audits.

9.3.2 Organisation & Rules

- Ensure by prequalification that designers and contractors are competent and can allocate sufficient resources to do the work.

- Make arrangements to publish that part of the SHE plan which describes the organisation and responsibilities of individuals, with regard to SHE issues. This should be clearly displayed on the site naming the Planning Supervisor and Principal Contractor.

- Ensure that all employees are made aware of site rules contained in the plan and are issued with copies where appropriate.

9.3.3   SHE Training

- Ensure that resources/facilities are provided and time is allowed for induction training, including SHE, of all staff/employees joining the project, together with site, job, trade training as necessary for safe completion of the work.

- Train planning staff to the level required for competent consideration of SHE in planning the work, including statutory duties.

- Set up a training record system covering induction, refresher, SHE and technical training for all staff.

9.3.4   Control of on-site design changes

- Plan constructability/buildability and hazards of construction ("HAZCON") reviews into the design process

- Plan hazard and operability reviews ("HAZOP") into the design process, including commissioning, start-up and shut-down.

- Plan demolition reviews into the design process to ensure that plant is capable of being demolished safely at the end of its useful life, considering especially radioactivity, chemical contamination, corrosion of structures.

9.3.5   Working Procedures

- Ensure that contractors comply with the health and safety plan and allocate the resources described in their tender.

- Develop the SHE plan for the project which ensures implementation of the conclusions reached during earlier risk assessments, e.g. "HAZCON" and addresses the SHE critical construction activities. Ensure that the plan is retained for use in compilation of the SHE file.

- Develop a site layout plan covering temporary accommodation, storage space, access routes for vehicles and pedestrians, pre-fab areas, crane assembly areas, emergency access routes.

- Identify SHE hazards which may be created for persons carrying out construction, commissioning maintenance and repair and the general public considering:

  - Abrasive wheels/disc cutters
  - Asbestos
  - Cartridge operated tools
  - Confined spaces
  - Contaminated ground
  - Crane operation
  - Demolition
  - Diving
  - Electricity
  - Excavations
  - Explosives
  - Falsework
  - Flammable materials

- Heavy lifts
- Hoists
- Lead burning
- Lifting gear
- Noise
- Pressure testing - hydraulic and pneumatic tests
- Radiography
- Roofwork/work at height
- Structural steelwork
- Transport
- Woodworking machinery
- Work over water
- Work within or adjacent to hazardous plant, e.g. operating chemical plant.

- Plan sequence of activities to eliminate hazards or avoid/minimise risks, consider all phases of the project including testing, commissioning, concurrent activities, live power or pressure systems.

- Prepare method statements for SHE significant activities.

- Identify statutory and other notifications and plan to submit ahead of need date. Where appropriate consult with the enforcing authority.

- Identify hazardous substances (which will be used/encountered after elimination and substitution with less hazardous materials has been considered) and plan communications and safety precautions.

- Identify requirements for permits to work/entry permits and build them into the schedule.

9.3.6 Procurement Controls

- Ensure that SHE requirements are passed on to suppliers of materials, plant and site work before contracts are placed.

- Consider priced "specification for safety" as part of the site work contract documentation.

9.3.7 Emergency Procedures

- Plan emergency procedures to cover: fire, excavation collapse, lifting gear failure, etc., requiring first aid, rescue, means of escape, ventilation, covering own/other employees and the general public.

- Allow time for training in emergency procedures

- Establish programme for testing of emergency procedures, including combined exercises with police, ambulance, fire brigade, local authority.

- Establish a contingency plan for corrective action. For example: to contain spillage of hazardous material.

9.3.8   Planned Inspections

Where the requirement for environmental monitoring has been determined (see Chapter 3).

- Set up an environmental monitoring programme; consider inside and outside the site boundary.

- Set up an inspection programme involving appropriate levels of staff and allowing adequate time/resource. The site rules and the agreed safe working methods incorporated in the SHE plan will be the basis of the inspection programme. Contractors and others working on the construction works should be monitored with regard to their compliance with the requirements of the plan and relevant statutory provisions.

Staff:	Medicals and health surveillance; protective clothing.
Emergency Equipment:	First aid, fire fighting, emergency escape.
Plant/Equipment including mobile plant and electrical installations:	Statutory and routine test/inspections.
Place of work:	Statutory notices; emergency exits; means of access; noise; fume; dust; contamination; exposure to wind, rain, ice.
Tasks:	Permits to work; safe working procedures; method statements; lifting studies.

9.3.9   SHE   Audits

- Set up an auditing programme involving appropriate levels of staff together with "independent" safety and other experts. Compliance with relevant statutory provisions and the health and safety plan will form the basis of the audits.

9.3.10   Incident and Accident Investigations

- Ensure that arrangements are in place before work starts to:

  - Report, record and analyse defined categories of accidents and incidents
  - Publicise root causes
  - Communicate/train to avoid recurrence
  - Monitor subsequent performance.

9.3.11   Recruitment and Placement

- Arrange recruitment evaluations/trade tests to enable competence to be judged including SHE aspects.

- Ensure that management/supervision are aware of their staff's capabilities and limitations enabling them to be allocated to appropriate tasks.

9.3.12 Occupational Health

- Establish arrangements for pre-job and regular medical examinations where required by construction activities.

- Establish arrangements for medical treatment arising from accidents, incidents or routine causes of ill-health.

- Produce method statements covering tasks involving hazardous materials that cannot be eliminated and for which there are no less hazardous substitutes.

- Arrange for noise surveys when justified by site activities or conditions on site resulting from adjacent activities.

9.3.13 Personal Protective Equipment (PPE)

- Ensure that the SHE plan specifies the requirements for personal protective equipment when on site.

- Allow time for issue/return of all personal protective equipment, whether personal issue or job specific.

- Ensure all the personal protective equipment needed for the project is available through an appropriate issuing facility with cleaning and maintenance capability.

9.3.14 Communications

- Build time into the programme to cover individual induction training and task instructions including compliance with method statements, statutory requirements and permits to work.

9.3.15 Meetings

- Build time into the programme to cover "tool-box talks" by supervisors on SHE and other matters.

9.3.16 Promotion

- Plan safety award/incentive schemes, poster displays, safety statistics displays, provision of management briefs for tool-box talks, etc., to extend over the life of the project.

9.3.17 Off-the-Job Safety

- Consider off-job as well as on-job safety publicity/promotions as part of the overall SHE plan for the project.

WORKED EXAMPLE   9.1

METHOD STATEMENTS

A Method Statement should be produced for each job that has inherent difficulties or significant SHE risks in its execution, either for those carrying out the work or those near the work location. One method statement should be produced covering quality, engineering and other aspects as well as SHE. These statements are often required by clients or regulatory authorities seeking assurance that the contractor intends tackling the work in a safe and professional manner and they should be produced automatically by contractors committed to the management of safety. Generalised method statements are sometimes submitted during the bid stage of a contract. These often prove to be of little use when it comes to carrying out the work and job specific method statements should always be provided where the hazards warrant a statement being produced at all. Frequently encountered jobs which usually justify method statements include, for example, structural steel erection, roof work and demolition. These are all jobs for which there is often no obvious safe means of access.

The date and origin of all method statements should be clearly shown.

Competent method statements will include the following key SHE features.

- Identification of the individual(s) who are responsible for ensuring compliance with the method statement, including deputising arrangements, e.g. named site agent and named supervisor as deputy.

- The qualifications/training/experience of those permitted to carry out the type of work and any special training for the specific job, e.g. labourer trained as dumper driver.

- Definition of the safe means of access to and from the work location, including permanent platforms, scaffolds (hand rails, toe boards, etc.) mobile towers. Requirements for barriers and notices to limit access to safe areas also needs to be spelt out.

- Identification of the safe access routes for plant and equipment, especially in congested areas and taking into account the need to maintain emergency access routes.

- Specification of the personal protective equipment and safety equipment to be used, e.g. safety harnesses (not belts) to be worn while aloft secured to pre-drilled anchor holes.

- Locations for off-job equipment and material storage and on-job lay-down, handling and security arrangements.

- Equipment required to carry out the work, how it will be provided and what inspections need to be carried out, including cranes, slings, etc.

- Definition of the sequence by which the work will be carried out with the aim of avoiding hazards and limiting any residual risk. Limitations to part-completed work, e.g. need for temporary supports, should be identified.

- The need for any temporary works to be provided and the responsibility for their competent design.

- Consideration of the impact of weather and limitations to working in adverse conditions.

- The method statement should generally indicate how risks are to be avoided, including those to other workers and the public at large, and to this end it is useful if it prohibits bad practices which are known to exist in the industry or can be anticipated on a particular job.

WORKED EXAMPLE   9.2

SHE ACTION PLANS

For most projects the SHE Action Plans may be incorporated into the overall SHE Plans described in Chapter 5. The aim of the Action Plan is to provide focused attention on specific aspects of the project.

SHE Action Plans should start by giving a brief outline of the Company's Safety, Health & Environment (SHE) policy and objectives. Measurable Goals or Targets can then be set for the specific project/contract which are clearly in support of the objectives.

For them to be effective the Action Plans must provide sufficient detail for people to understand clearly and unambiguously what they are expected to do in order to achieve the targets. The Action Plans cannot be expected to succeed unless they are COMMUNICATED and EXPLAINED to all the individuals involved and accepted by them.

The plans should address the key areas where action is required to:

•   Minimise the risk of personal injury or hazard to health

•   Ensure the security of people, information and material property

•   Protect the environment.

Good SHE Action Plans will be wholly relevant to the activities of the individuals expected to follow them and involve people at every level of the organisation in such a way that support from the top is clear to all. They must cover the full range of activities under the management of the organisation issuing the plans.

The plans themselves often run to several pages, but if they are to be put into practice with the minimum of effort they need to be supported at the time of issue with briefing papers covering, for example, induction training, tool box talks, report forms.

Key areas to be included in an Action Plan can be selected from the check-list of items in the Pre-construction and Construction Planning section. It should explain WHO should do WHAT and WHEN the action should be taken. Commitment to the plan will be increased if the reason WHY the action is required is also explained. Project SHE Action Plans need to cover all phases of the project while Contract or Site Action Plans cover only one part of the whole project.

An effective presentation of an Action Plan, which allows a degree of discretion over timing and provides clear visual indication of achievement, is shown in Tables 9.1 and 9.2 (courtesy of Eden Construction Ltd). The range of options (shown across the top) are intended to be colour coded for a specific contract and the time plan is marked with the appropriate colour when the action has been taken. This presentation makes it easy to monitor progress against the plan and is particularly suitable for a site situation. These forms assume a 'stand-alone' Action Plan, and the format may need to be adapted to suit incoporation into the overall SHE Plan.

On completion of the work there should be a review to establish just how well the Action Plan worked and to provide information for future improved plans.

TABLE 9.1 CONTRACT SHE ACTION PLAN

SHE SAMPLING

Specific safety sampling One/Week by Site Agent	Plant Documentation e.g. Test Certs	Material Storage & Stacking	Safety Helmets	Condition of Welfare Facilities	Hand Tools Condition & Use	Eye Protection Condition & Use	Excavation Safety	Site Tidiness	Edge Protection	LPG Storage & Use

Specific Safety sampling One/Week By Site Agent	Cartridge Multi Tool Storage & Use	Power Tools Maintenance & Use	Noise Control & Protective Defenders	Painting Safety	Plant & Vehicle Condition/Driver Competence	Wood Working Machines Condition & Use	Steel Structure Erection Procedure Compliance	COSHH Knowledge & Compliance	Hoists Condition & Use	Use of Bitumen Boilers	Fire Fighting Equipment

Acknowledgement: Eden Construction Group

127

TABLE 9.2 CONTRACT SHE ACTION PLAN (Continued)

SHE MANAGEMENT COMMITMENT

	Statutory Notices Displayed	Scaffold Toe-Boards	Scaffold Guard Rails	Scaffold Loading Bay Guard Rails	Ladder Access	Scaffold Ties and Bracing	Roofwork Safety Compliance	Sub-Contractors Working Practices	Demolition Safe System of Work Compliance	Plant Operators Safe Operating Practices
Safety Adviser Fortnightly Inspection										
Site Agent Tool Box Talks										
Contracts Manager Fortnightly Inspection										
Construction Director Monthly Inspection										
Managing Director Quarterly Inspection										
Video Showing Every 4 months										
On Site Safety Training										
Poster Campaign 1 Poster Changed Every Week										
Site Agent Fortnightly Inspection										

Acknowledgement: Eden Construction Group

TABLE 9.2   CONTRACT SHE ACTION PLAN   (Continued)

SHE MANAGEMENT COMMITMENT (Continued)

	Compressed Air Safety Tools, Fittings & Compressor	Safety Induction Review of Employees Knowledge	First Aid Provisions	Children's Safety Prevention Reduction of Risk	Protection of the Public	Lifting Operations Safe Systems of Work	Manual Handling of Loads Proper Assessment	Respiratory Protection Use & Cars	Piling Operations Safe System of Work
Safety Advisor Fortnightly Inspection									
Site Agent Tool Box Talks									
Contracts Manager Fortnightly Inspection									
Construction Director Monthly Inspection									
Managing Director Quarterly Inspection									
Video Showing Every 4 months									
On Site Safety Training									
Poster Campaign 1 Poster Changed Every Week									
Site Agent Fortnightly Inspection									

Acknowledgement: Eden Construction Group

129

CHAPTER 10

CONSTRUCTION

10.1   Introduction

The primary aim of SHE management is to provide a working environment within which construction activities can proceed in a safe manner.

The objective of this chapter is to provide a consistent framework that can be used to monitor and control SHE during the construction phase.

The framework developed in this chapter should allow the parties involved in construction activities to answer with confidence the questions:

"Are the construction activities complying with the agreed SHE plans?"

"What can be done to improve SHE performance?"

10.2   Construction - Identification of Major SHE Issues

The major SHE issues that are associated with the construction phase of the project can be summarised as:

- Client, Planning Supervisor and Principal Contractor SHE systems
  - in place prior to mobilisation

- Client, Planning Supervisor and Principal Contractor compliance with the SHE plan
  - SHE monitoring by Principal Contractor
  - SHE monitoring by Client (or agent)

- SHE File
  - Planning Supervisor to collate SHE File
  - Principal Contractor, contractors and sub-contractors to provide information

- Level of Client (or Client's agent) supervision
  - Client supervision must not relieve the Principal Contractor or contractors of their SHE responsibilities.

- Client and Principal Contractor SHE management structures
  - In place prior to mobilisation
  - Line responsibility for SHE
  - SHE professionals
  - First aiders etc

- Construction SHE audits
  - Spot checks
  - Full SHE audits
  - Corrective action
  - Review and feedback

- Project execution and SHE performance monitoring
  - SHE statistics for project
  - Frequency and effectiveness of SHE meetings
  - Regular SHE reporting (at site progress meetings) including near miss incidents and other learning events

- On the job SHE training

- Construction SHE requirements
  - Work permit systems
  - Commissioning and handover
  - Correct execution of agreed method statements
  - Use of plant and equipment
  - Access and egress
  - Operation in confined spaces
  - Protection of existing services
  - Protection from buried and overhead power lines

- Promotion of SHE to employees

- Duty of care to the General Public
  - Site hoardings
  - Access ways and general protection
  - Dust and dirt
  - Protective scaffold fans (screens)

- Contractors and sub-contractor compliance with Principal Contractor SHE plan
  - Use of casual labour

10.3   Check List

To aid the formation and development of a construction SHE framework the following checklist has been developed. The checklist is not exhaustive and particular attention should be paid to project specific SHE issues.

The Project Team can comprise any or all of the Client, his Site Representative, the Design Team, the Planning Supervisor and the Principal Contractor, depending on the nature and complexity of the project.

10.3.1   Management and Leadership

- A senior member of the Principal Contractor's organisation should be assigned overall responsibility for construction SHE.

- The role, authority and reporting lines of the SHE advisers should be clearly defined, down to all contractors and sub-contractors.

- The Project Team should install appropriate systems to allow effective SHE management.

- These management systems should address:
  - SHE training
  - Ongoing monitoring and inspection of construction work
  - Auditing and periodic inspection

- Construction organisation including lines of responsibility and communication
- Enforcement of SHE rules and procedures
- Feedback of SHE issues to all employees
- SHE co-ordination between all parties, including sub-contractors and suppliers
- Investigation and reporting of accidents and incidents
- Liaison with regulatory and statutory authorities.

- The senior members of the Project Team should clearly demonstrate leadership, commitment and support for SHE, leading by example.

- The Project Team should demonstrate appropriate access to expertise and advice on SHE issues; including hazard assessment, legislation and risk prevention.

- The Project Team should establish and maintain overall site SHE policy including the provision and use of common facilities, plant, equipment, emergency procedures and services.

- The Project Team should maintain good working relationships with appointed safety representatives and/or safety committees.

10.3.2   Organisation and Rules

- The Project Team must demonstrate that site organisation together with SHE rules and procedures are in place prior to commencement on site.

- The Project Team must demonstrate that all personnel are fully aware of and understand the implications of relevant SHE policy.

- The Project Team must demonstrate its ability to monitor regularly and ensure compliance with their construction SHE plan.

- The Project Team's organisation and SHE management system should allow the updating of rules and procedures to match the construction phase and the changing SHE issues.

10.3.3   SHE Training

- The Principal Contractor should confirm and demonstrate their policy on SHE induction and training:
  - For new employees and for employees new to the type of operations or site
  - At the commencement of construction activities
  - Specific training for each level of employee, highlighting responsibilities and statutory requirements.

- The Principal Contractor should identify and provide specialist SHE training where appropriate, such as:
  - Operation and maintenance of plant and equipment
  - Handling of hazardous materials
  - Work in confined spaces
  - Requirements of agreed method statements and working practices (work permit etc).

- The Principal Contractor should carry out regular reviews of the training programme to ensure that the training needs of the SHE plan and current legislative and policy requirements are being met.

10.3.4 Control of on-site design changes

- The Project Team should demonstrate their ability to manage the SHE implications of design and specification changes.

10.3.5 Working Procedures

- The Principal Contractor shall establish safe and effective working procedures and practices based on a systematic analysis of the construction tasks (and the associated SHE issues) and allowance of sufficient time for task stages.

- The Principal Contractor must ensure that all SHE hazards have been identified and that safe systems of working have been put in place.

- The Principal Contractor must work to the agreed programme schedule of work and agreed method statements. Where changes in scope or procedures are necessary, the Principal Contractor must ensure that the appropriate SHE systems are put in place, and all parties informed.

- Where "high risk" construction activities are necessary, the Principal Contractor must prepare a detailed written SHE procedure and install the necessary control and management systems (such as permit to work systems).

10.3.6 Procurement Controls

- The Principal Contractor shall ensure that all site purchases and supplier orders comply with the agreed SHE plan and relevant legislation.

- Any information regarding site purchases of supplier orders that has SHE significance should be communicated to the Planning Supervisor for inclusion in the Safety File.

10.3.7 Emergency Procedures

- The Principal Contractor must demonstrate that emergency procedures have been developed and are in place prior to commencement of construction activities, including the necessary interface with emergency services (both internal and external).

- The emergency procedures should be published and distributed to all parties, including outside bodies where appropriate, prior to site activities .

- The Principal Contractor is to ensure that all staff are given adequate training in emergency procedures. Where appropriate an emergency co-ordinator should be appointed with suitable responsibilities and authority.

- Emergency procedures must be rehearsed regularly.

- Alarms and systems must be tested regularly.

- Emergency equipment and plant should be regularly inspected and maintained.

- Ensure liaison with outside emergency services, hospitals and doctors.

10.3.8 Planned Inspections

- The SHE inspections are to ensure continued and satisfactory SHE performance.

- Planned and systematic SHE inspections are to be carried out using trained personnel. Frequency of the inspections will recognise the nature of the construction activities, the hazards present and the performance on the site.

- The Principal Contractor's SHE management systems shall describe corrective actions required in the event of non compliance with SHE Plan.

- The Principal Contractor will ensure that statutory examinations, inspections and notifications for items such as plant, equipment, excavations, medical facilities, etc, are carried out at the required intervals.

- Records, certificates and registers are to be kept, where appropriate, in a central location. They are to be monitored regularly to ensure that they comply with SHE and regulatory requirements.

10.3.9 SHE Audits

- The Principal Contractor shall ensure that SHE monitoring forms a regular part of site SHE activities.

- The Principal Contractor shall periodically audit the SHE management systems and procedures to ensure the goals of the SHE plan are being achieved. Where necessary corrective actions are to be detailed and implemented.

10.3.10 Incident / Accident Investigations

- The Principal Contractor, through the SHE management systems and procedures, shall ensure that all accidents and incidents are reported and investigated. The accident/incident investigation procedures should:
  - Comply with appropriate statutory reporting requirements
  - Be carried out by competent, trained staff
  - Follow agreed methods and procedures
  - Require senior management attention and action
  - Provide feedback of root causes and allow learning
  - Allow the compilation of suitable statistics
  - Determine trends and detail corrective actions.

- Recommendations from accident investigations should be implemented to an agreed schedule. Safety procedures, practices and training should be modified to prevent recurrence of incidents.

- Near miss incidents should be investigated and communicated as learning events.

10.3.11 Recruitment and Placement

- The Principal Contractor should arrange the necessary induction training and instruction for all new employees and transfers.

- The Principal Contractor's recruitment practice should recognise SHE criteria in the screening and selection of employees.

- Site personnel who carry out specialised tasks such as crane driving, banksman, scaffolding, etc, must be properly trained and their competency regularly monitored.

10.3.12 Occupational Health

- The Principal Contractor should ensure that employees undergo pre-employment and regular medical examinations where appropriate.

- The Principal Contractor should carry out reviews of work practices to eliminate or reduce hazardous conditions.

- The Principal Contractor is to ensure that hazardous substances are identified, assessments made and procedures for use are prepared before work commences.

10.3.13 Personal Protective Equipment (PPE)

- The Principal Contractor must demonstrate adequate management systems for the provision and use of personal protective equipment. Items that need to be identified include:
  - Procedures for identifying PPE requirements for the project
  - Employee instruction in use, storage and maintenance
  - Recording issue and use of equipment
  - Satisfactory inventory management systems for PPE.

10.3.14 Communications

- The Principal Contractor is to ensure effective communication of SHE procedures and policies within the team and to all employees. Specific items that should be identified include:
  - Role of supervisors and health and safety officers
  - Method of communication (Tool-box talks etc)
  - Feedback from employees.

10.3.15 Meetings

- The Principal Contractor should hold planned and informal group meetings with the Project Team on a regular basis. Participants should include managers, supervisors and staff.

- Regular on-site project SHE meetings with all relevant parties attending (e.g. client, contractors, sub-contractors teams, safety advisers and, where appropriate, appointed trade union representatives) should be convened.

- A suitable agenda should be developed and circulated prior to this meeting. Planned meetings should be minuted with actions summarised and implemented and progress monitored by the Principal Contractor.

10.3.16 Promotion

- Safe behaviour and a proactive SHE culture should be promoted throughout the construction phase using:
  - Management/leadership
  - Enforcement of SHE procedures
  - Tool box talks
  - Posters
  - Displays
  - Safety Representatives and employee participation
  - Videos
  - Competitions
  - Notice boards displaying SHE statistics
  - Information handouts
  - Promotional campaigns (using actual site incidents as source material).
  - Involvement of SHE professionals
  - Employee participation in the promotion of the SHE culture.

10.3.17 Off the Job Safety

- Encourage SHE awareness outside of the work place, for the benefit of both employee and employer.

- As part of the SHE programme highlight off-the-job risks and foster a positive attitude towards high safety standards and make safety awareness a matter of habit.

WORKED EXAMPLE 10.1

SHE INDUCTION TRAINING PROGRAMME

This programme is for SHE training of direct employees. Variations may be required for others involved on the site.

Introduction

- Set up induction record system for all staff.

- Induction training should be carried out before commencing and should take into account skill, tasks and site environment.

- Draw up a check list of points that need to be covered, and leave a space for the trainee to sign that he/she has been informed.

- Ensure that more than one person is able to conduct induction training, so that there is cover at holiday periods, sickness, etc.

- If the employee is new to the type of work that he or she will do, or to the sort of environment that the work will take place in, ensure that adequate training is provided, and that adequate time is given for this task.

Content

- Ensure that trainees are aware of their own and their employer's responsibilities under the law and the Company Safety Policy.

- Ensure that trainees are aware of the content of the relevant sections of the SHE Plan, and notified of the Planning Supervisor and Principal Contractor for the project.

- Ensure that trainees understand how to deal with hazardous substances which will be used or encountered on the construction work.

- Collect any forms/information needed, including SHE information.

- Issue any company SHE literature.

- Issue any personal protective equipment needed, make sure it fits properly, make aware of how and when to wear it, how to look after it and to report defects.

- Explain any security systems. Issue with any passes/permits needed.

- Notify trainees of emergency plan, and when on shared sites, ensure that client or occupants emergency evacuation systems are explained and understood.

- Establish whereabouts of first-aid facilities and show them who is the first aider(s).

- Emphasise the need and explain how to report all accidents.

- Identify areas where smoking is permitted.

- Identify location of notice boards.

- Inform of any standards of safety, health, hygiene, etc, expected by the company.

- Explain arrangements and need for good housekeeping.

- Explain that horseplay is not tolerated.

- Establish that there is time to enable the work to be done safely.

- Ensure that a trainee knows what equipment cannot be operated with his/her lack of experience.

- Explain permit-to-work system and method statement(s).

- Inform about risks of the work and the precautions to be taken.

- Emphasise that most accidents occur during a person's first fortnight on a new site.

- Identify the most frequent accidents for the work, and explain how they can be prevented.

- Explain layout of site/project and, if possible, conduct a tour of work place, noting dangers, exits, etc.

- Ensure site management hierarchy is explained and introduce employee to his/her supervisor.

Follow-up

- The supervisor should carry out an induction programme follow-up to make sure questions can be answered, comments made, after a week has passed since the first induction training.

WORKED EXAMPLE 10.2

SAFETY MOTIVATION PROGRAMME

Background

- Safety is a form of self preservation. However, different individuals have various perceptions about risk and safety.

- Motivation is a complex issue, but is enhanced through participation, commitment, communication, achievement and feedback.

Motivation

- Establish attainable goals and give encouragement to motivate people over a long period.

- Generally, prize money is not considered to be a suitable reward for motivation, whereas public recognition, authority and promotion are.

- Set up targets and charts to plot the safety progress. They must, however, be updated regularly to keep employees interested. However, if too much importance is given to a 'clean' chart it may lead to the unlawful non-reporting of accidents. Encourage the reporting of dangerous situations to supervisors.

- Ensure that employees realise the cost of an accident, in terms of finance, lives, etc.

- Ensure that employees are aware that their workplace should not be assumed to be safe and that regular safety checks are to be carried out.

- Encourage safe working by making it the easy option and rewarding safe performance.

- Ensure that safety posters are renewed frequently, so that they do not become old and 'part of the furniture' to give maximum motivation.

- Managers and Supervisors should be reviewed by senior staff on SHE issues.

Safety Officers, Safety Advisers and Safety Representatives

- Advice is taken more readily if given by a member of ones own group or an individual of prestige.

- Ensure that safety representatives bring safety into a central position of work practice to keep it in the minds of the workers. Employees should get into the habit of working safely.

- The safety committee should consist of the site management, safety officers, safety advisers and safety representatives where applicable and may provide a useful motivational tool.

- Good communication is essential for safety motivation - assign responsibility and give accountability to the safety representative.

- Allocate time for the members of the safety committee to inspect the site regularly.

Example by Management

- Ensure that management, while on site, sets a good example of being safe - in personal protective equipment use, words and actions.

- Motivation can only be achieved if management shows enthusiasm/commitment.

- Management should be concerned with motivating people to an appropriate level of performance.

- Ensure that managers facilitate a good relationship between the individual and the work to obtain maximum motivation.

- Set up a safety motivated site where management is fully involved in the safety effort and every employee is committed to good safety performance.

- Every aspect of safety reflects top management's motivation and its influence on those who are managed.

Success

- It is difficult to quantify the success of safety motivation. It is impossible to predict what the accident figures would have been in an unmotivated situation. One can only compare with previous results.

WORKED EXAMPLE   10.3

PERMIT TO WORK SYSTEMS

Introduction

- Set up a permit to work system for any job where there is a risk, e.g. non-routine work where more than one group of workers are interacting on a job.

- Recognise which type of permit is needed. The following is a list of the main examples:

  'Hot' and 'Cold' work permit
  Electrical Work work permit
  Confined Spaces entry permit
  Pressure Test permit
  Ionising Radiation or Radiography permit
  Hazardous Dust permit
  Release of Flammable/Toxic Liquid or Gas permit
  Erection/Dismantling of Scaffolding Over Water permit
  Excavation permit
  Mechanical permit.

- Some situations require all work to be covered by a permit.

- Establish if more than one permit is needed, or if the whole aspect is covered by the permit used. If necessary, write additional notes.

- A permit to work helps to set up 'systems of work' that control the inherent risks in the job.

- The permit to work document should incorporate check lists of all the preparatory steps, and when completed, should contain a list of all of the equipment necessary to do the job. It should clearly identify the scope of work which must not be exceeded.

- Identify the risks of the work at a preliminary meeting before the permit is issued. Make sure time is given to writing the permit. Check any reports, drawings and method statements relating to the work.

- Identify a way of warning everyone in the vicinity of the work that a permit will be issued.

- Ensure that the permit identifies hazards and establishes precautions that need to be taken (e.g. safety equipment, lone worker alarms, warning signs).

- Permits should only be issued and accepted by technically competent persons who are familiar with the system and equipment and are authorised in writing by the employers to issue/accept such permits. They should realise the responsibilities they have.

- The permit must be properly authorised and accepted before work commences.

- Ensure that a competent and authorised person issues the permit to a second person who is competent and authorised to receive it.

- As far as is reasonably possible, only the issuer of the permit can cancel it and the permit cannot be cancelled, altered or overridden by any other person (no matter how senior) except in a shift work situation when responsibility is formally handed over to a second individual.

- Permit to work certificates should be of the 'no carbon required' variety, and each set should have a specific serial number. One should be placed in a plastic cover and displayed near the place of work. Another should be retained in the permit book until the work has been completed and the permit signed off. A copy should also be distributed to the engineering department, or whatever the company requires.

Procedure

- Information should be precise, detailed and accurate on the permit. Limits should be defined and not exceeded. Any changes need a new permit.

- Depending on the nature of the work, the permit may be limited to a certain length of time, to make sure that the situation is reassessed, or training given to new workers. Limits may be 24 hours, length of shift etc.

- If the time runs out, a new permit has to be written or the existing permit revalidated by the issuing authority. The work should not be carried out on an invalid permit. This is to ensure that conditions have not changed.

- Ensure adherence to the work areas specified on the permit.

- Any age limits or training needed for the work should be specified.

- Any switching off/isolation of equipment that is required should be done so that it is impossible to switch on etc., before work is completed. If necessary use lock switches with two keys, one to be kept by the issuer of the permit and one by the receiver. Make sure keys are not inadvertently left in/by locks.

- Check that anyone who may be affected by the permit is notified prior to work commencing and that anyone whose work is covered by a permit has seen it. If necessary list the number of people who can work under the permit - as a safety check and to make sure adequate equipment is provided.

- The work must stop if conditions change.

- Ensure that workers realise that a permit overrides everything else concerned with the work. However, the permit is automatically suspended upon the sounding of emergency alarms and must be checked with the issuing authority before recommencing work.

- Ensure that rescue drills are understood before operations commence.

Completion

- Checks should be made to make sure that the areas are tidy and that no workers remain, before the permit is signed off/cancelled.

- After the work is completed any warning signs should be removed.

- After work has been finished the permit should be signed by the receiver to say work has been completed or stopped and signed by the issuer to say the permit is cancelled and all equipment and keys have been returned to the permit issuer.

- All issued copies of the permit, should be returned to the issuing authority for destruction when work is complete.

- All aspects of permits issued should be monitored by the issuing authority at regular intervals during their validity period.

CHAPTER 11

PRECOMMISSIONING AND COMMISSIONING

11.1 Introduction

Commissioning covers the activities required to bring plant, equipment, building management systems, etc, to the state of operability defined by the Designer/Engineer.

The SHE requirements for this activity will have been identified both by the client and the designer and detailed in the project SHE plan, during the planning phase of the project (see chapter 9).

This chapter identifies the key SHE issues that must be considered during the on-site precommissioning and commissioning phase of the project. A checklist of items to be considered has been developed. The chapter concludes with a worked example.

The framework detailed in this chapter should allow the parties involved in commissioning to answer with confidence the question:

"How can the commissioning phase be managed such that the SHE goals detailed in the Project SHE plan are met?"

11.2 Commissioning - Identification of the Key SHE issues

The health, safety and environmental information already documented in the SHE Plan and collated for the SHE File will be useful reference material for the commissioning team.

The results of the commissioning tests both as regards sequence of testing and method of obtaining results will be required to be documented and forwarded to the operator of the plant e.g. as part of the SHE File.

The key SHE issues that should be considered during the on-site commissioning phase can be summarised as follows.

- Are intentions in the SHE plan still valid?

- On site management and organisation

  - Management of interfaces

- Commissioning Procedures

  - Commissioning sequence
  - SHE critical stages
  - Hazardous / Non Hazardous areas
  - Emergency procedures
  - Phased commissioning

- Concurrent Operations

  - Commissioning / Construction
  - Hazards to other parties
  - Management of, and communication at, the interfaces
  - Adjacent plant operations

- Maintenance of proper records

  - Prioritised checklist of SHE critical activities
  - Input to SHE File.

- Ratification of Design Criteria

  - Expected vs Actual performance
  - Assessment of SHE risks
  - On-site modifications
  - Feedback and communication to client for operation and maintenance and to designer for future designs

11.3   Check List

A checklist of the SHE items to be considered is presented below.

11.3.1   Management and Leadership

- The Commissioning team leader should also be assigned overall responsibility for SHEissues.
- The interfaces and SHE relationships must be identified between all concerned parties.
- The commissioning team should install appropriate systems and procedures to allow effective SHE management. These should address:

  - Organisational responsibilities
  - Definition of SHE rules and controls
  - Area subject to commissioning
  - Lines of communication
  - Areas of SHE responsibility
  - SHE monitoring and inspection of commissioning activities
  - SHE training for all employees.

- Identify SHE issues relevant to commissioning.
- Ensure time has been allowed for SHE inspections.
- Confirm SHE activities have been allowed for in commissioning programme.
- Produce procedures detailing the operational sequence.
- Define the handover point for SHE responsibility.
- Define the point at which normal operators procedures will apply such as:

  - permits to work
  - erection clearance certificate
  - plant handover documents.

11.3.2 Working Procedures

- List and prioritise risks associated with the operation of the tests and the methods of obtaining the test results. Identify the SHE hazards and assess the risks, (see modified HAZOP technique in the worked example)

- Establish the schedule of tests and programme for execution, recognising SHE issues (including the application of safer test methods).

- Designate the terminal points of the tests.

- Identify the SHE risks to team personnel and persons not directly involved with the commissioning.

- Ensure that SHE hazard assessments are in place for issues such as:

  - hazardous substances
  - noise.

- Plan activities to minimise/avoid exposure to SHE hazards:

  - precautions to be taken (e.g. emergency stops, chocks, valve positions, regulators)

  - control measures to be provided (e.g. to prevent exceeding safe limits).

  - Define the areas of plant that require a control document in accordance with the organisational rules and SHE plan, e.g. Permit to Work.

- Define the training requirements with respect to the hazards.

- Detail the personal protective equipment for the tests.

- Ensure identified personal protective equipment is readily available on site.

- Produce noise assessments for the operation of the plant.
  Emergency Procedures

- Ensure that health controls, in respect of process gases/fluids are in place for all tests e.g. such as water treatment, exhaust emissions.

- Ensure that emergency engineering controls for the tests are available or in position.

- Determine access requirements to enable the test results to be obtained safely and personnel to exit safely.

- Ensure that all exit routes including emergency exit routes are clear.

- Check that all communication systems are functional including backup systems.

- Ensure test materials are dealt with, and disposed of, in accordance with the SHE plan.

- Check that emergency facilities are in place.

- Check that fire precautions are in place or available.

- Check fire alarms are operational.

- Issue all members of the commissioning team with the fire plan.

- Check first aid facilities are in place or available.

- Check first aid alarms are operational.

- Ensure that equipment is available to remove injured personnel from high level and basement areas.

- Issue all members of the commissioning team with the first aid plan.
- Issue all members of the commissioning team with the procedure in the event of a spillage/uncontrolled release of an environmental controlled substance.

  - Communication with internal and external emergency services

- Prepare, communicate and rehearse emergency procedures.

11.3.3 Planned Inspections

- Verify SHE programme and physical conditions. Are SHE assumptions still valid?

- Detail the inspections to be carried out prior to the start of testing. A system of auditing the SHE controls should be defined and disseminated to the team.

- Detail the SHE inspections to be carried out during the tests, such as:

  - safety precautions (e.g. the position of on/off controls and switches)

  - criteria to be satisfied before inspection can go ahead e.g. pressure held for a given time then reduced to a defined level before inspection carried out.

- Detail the final SHE inspection after tests.

- General inspection by safety co-ordinator in accordance with SHE assessment. Ensure inspections occur with sufficient frequency.

- Reporting procedure on hazardous conditions to be implemented along with re-assessment of SHE procedures.

  - requirements for remedial action.

- Tests should be monitored and recorded throughout for compliance to SHE standards and procedures.

- Maintenance operations which are to be undertaken by operational personnel rated as being practical and safe.

- Any inadequacy of guarding arrangements should be recorded and actions taken to rectify.

- Modifications to the plant as a result of tests should be validated, approved and recorded.

11.3.4   Incident/Accident Investigations

- Establish procedures for investigation and reporting of all accidents/incidents and dangerous occurrences which cause loss, potential near-misses and actual injury.

11.3.5   Communication

- Ensure any residual risks identified during commissioning are forwarded to the Planning Supervisor for inclusion in the SHE File. Ultimately, this file will be issued to the final operators of the plant/building.

11.3.6   Meetings

- Regular SHE meetings should be held to:

    - Evaluate operational effectiveness of SHE controls during commissioning

    - Review accidents and incidents

    - Provide a forum for the discussion of safety problems with construction team members

    - Review operating and maintenance procedures

    - Develop checklists and action lists in response to evaluation of ongoing commissioning activities.

WORKED EXAMPLE 11.1

COMMISSIONING OF A PROCESS/PRODUCTION PLANT

The Project Designer should have prepared the procedures for commissioning the plant to achieve the objectives of the project. These procedures are to: (a) ensure the correct sequential operation of the plant, (b) define the tests to be completed and the parameters for acceptance of the tests.

A number of problem areas can occur with this approach in respect to SHE.

- The original objectives for a project are often modified due to a number of factors; pressure on the completion date, the lack of finance, experience from similar projects, availability of new materials, improved testing, machinery/techniques and changes in personnel.

- The access to the plant is difficult to predict due to the stage at which commissioning commences, the other work taking place adjacent or on the plant to be commissioned and the number of temporary working platforms remaining in situ.

- The planned sequential operation of the plant may not be possible or desirable due to changes in design or final layout. The feedback of information is often poor to non-existent, not only through carelessness but the designer may have completed his part of the project and not be involved. These changes should be notified to the Planning Supervisor in order to update the SHE Plan and subsequently the commissioning procedure.

- There may be parts of the project that can only be detailed at a late stage due to ongoing tests of suitable materials or results from the performance of other sections of the plant. Similarly with changes in statutory legislation e.g. operational exposure limits, noise limits, waste discharges.

- The plant is usually built

  - in geographical areas

  - by contractor discipline, e.g. civil, mechanical

Commissioning is usually by process system which may cross several plant areas and require all disciplines to be completed. The problem is often most acute with services systems which are first to be commissioned and then used to commission the rest of the plant.

Due to the above problems it is essential that the Commissioning Team Leader undertakes to carry out risk assessment with respect to the commissioning procedures ideally with the original designer and operational specialists. It must not only consider the plant process but the safe systems of work for the commissioning personnel.

WORKED EXAMPLE 11.2

MODIFIED HAZOP TECHNIQUE

The examination procedure uses a series of questions based on guide words to test the integrity of each part of the design to every theoretical deviation.

This results in a number of possible causes, and their operational consequences and leads to actions required for safeguarding the plant and the personnel involved before commissioning of the plant commences.

Although the report from such a HAZOP review may be time consuming to produce, the actual process of asking and arriving at a suitable response is easily achieved, assuming the panel contains the appropriate persons with authority to make such decisions.

This HAZOP study may differ from the original design HAZOP because of the piecemeal way the process plant or building services are commissioned.

TABLE OF GUIDE WORDS

Guide Word	Deviations	Possible Causes	Consequences	Action Required
None	No Flow, quantity, temperature, pressure etc when there should be			
Reverse	Opposite effect to design intention			
More	Increase in flow, quantity, temperature, pressure, current, voltage, radiation compared with design			
Less	Decrease in flow, quantity, temperature, pressure, current, voltage, radiation compared with design			
Part of	Change in the composition of the system, component ratio change, component missing			
As Well As	Additions to the composition of the system, contamination, moisture, vapour, viscosity			
Other Than	Changes from normal operation start up, shutdown, uprating, low late running, alternative operation mode, failure of plant services, maintenance			

The guide words above are broadly used, and when applied to the plant items, it is often necessary to use them in conjunction with the term of a physical property.

But this process can also be used for the protection of personnel as the guide word and the deviation as one of the properties shown below.

Examples of such properties that it may be useful to consider are:

Physical

Flow, Pressure, Temperature, Capacity, Quantity, Viscosity, Moisture, Contamination, Force, Radioactivity,

Protection of Personnel

Access, Training, Procedures, Personal Protection, Communications.

CHAPTER 12

HANDOVER

12.1   Introduction

The SHE requirements for this activity will have been identified and detailed in the SHE plan, during the planning phase of the project (see chapter 9).

This chapter identifies the key issues that must be considered during the handover phase of the project. The handover phase consists of commissioning certificates, operating instructions, maintenance instructions which will be collated into a SHE File for the Project. A checklist of items to be considered has been developed. The chapter concludes with a worked example based on commissioning certification.

The framework detailed in this chapter should allow the parties involved in commissioning to answer with confidence the question:

"How can the handover phase be managed such that the SHE goals detailed in the SHE plan are met?"

12.2   Handover - Identification of the Key SHE Issues

The key SHE issues that should be considered during the handover phase of the project are:

- Are the SHE intentions in the project SHE plan still valid and acceptable to the client?

- Is the design criteria along with the record drawings available to the client?

- Have the materials used along with their data sheets been itemised?

- Is the type of operational and maintenance equipment clearly shown along with the requisite operating instructions?

- On site management and organisation

    - Management of interfaces-organisational responsibilities and structure clearly defined?

- Continuity of SHE

    - Phased handover
    - SHE critical stages
    - Emergency procedures

- Concurrent Operations

    - Handover/Commissioning/Construction
    - Hazards to other parties
    - Management of and communication at the interfaces

- Documentation

    - Prioritised checklist of SHE critical activities

    - Maintenance of proper records

- Communication

  - Feedback and communication from all phases, that could have SHE implications for operational phase.

12.3   Checklist

A checklist of other items is presented below:

- Ensure the SHE information has been defined and agreed between Client, Planning Supervisor, professional advisers and Principal Contractor. This information to be included in the SHE File including the operating instructions and maintenance procedures.

- Agree formal handover procedures

  - Phased handover
  - Notification to all personnel
  - Notification to external bodies

- Issue final, updated SHE Plan for the project

- Define points of isolation for plant that is to be operated by the Client's/owner's staff

  - Clearly demonstrate the system interface points

- Identify SHE issues

  - Live services
  - Hazardous materials
  - Hazardous areas
  - Fire precautions
  - Statutory documentation

- Define health controls for personnel

- Define environmental controls

- Limits on dry waste disposal, air discharges and effluent discharges

- Detail SHE training requirements for operators and maintenance personnel

- Ensure SHE control procedures are in place and satisfactorily completed

  - Work on commissioned plant
  - Work on operational plant
  - Training
  - Maintenance
  - Operation of plant

WORKED EXAMPLE 12.1

TYPICAL CONTENT FOR A HEALTH AND SAFETY FILE
(Based on handover of an administration building)

A)   Structural Requirements

1) Drawings
2) Design Loadings
3) Demolition Method Statement (Specific design criteria)
4) Post Tensioned Slabs demolition requirements.

B)   Access Systems

1) Roof
2) Windows
   - 2.1) Offices
   - 2.2) Atrium
   - 2.3) Curtain Walling
   - 2.4) Lift Shafts

C)   Confined Spaces

1) Plantrooms
2) Manhole Ducts
3) Pump Chambers
4) Plenum Chambers
5) Service Risers
6) Service Voids
7) Cableways

D)   Test and Inspection Procedures

1) Safety harness attachment points and equipment.
2) Pressurised systems
3) Lifting Equipment
4) Effluent/drainage systems

E)   Operation/Maintenance Permits to Work Areas.

1) Window cleaning/maintenance
2) Roof
3) Plantrooms
4) Service risers
5) Raised Floors
6) Suspended Ceilings
7) Lift Motor room
8) Manholes
9) Information Technology equipment/rooms
10) Pump Chambers

F)   Maintenance Procedures/Frequency of Plant & Equipment

1) Removal and Dismantling of bulk plant and equipment:
   e.g. Roof ventilation equipment, basement heating/water equipment
2) Loading restrictions of floors/roofs/external roads/car parking areas.
3) Glazing replacement procedure : atrium/offices.
4) Exterior fabric cleaning and repair.

5) Demolition
6) Cable routes repair/additional cables.
7) Loading bay restrictions/operations.
8) Fire Hydrants /hose reels /fire extinguishers
9) Emergency Lighting

G) Construction Materials

1) Sealants and gaskets
2) Paints
3) Insulation
4) Oils
5) Glues
6) Lubricants
7) Building fabric e.g. plasters/flooring/concrete/brickwork.

H) Pressurised Systems/Vessels

J) Emergency Procedures

1) Building Evacuation-Muster Points
2) Building Evacuation-Disabled Persons, visitors contractors.
3) Protected routes/security systems
4) Fire Alarms
5) Fire Fighting Equipment
6) Access routes for fire fighting appliances and personnel.

K) Environmental Issues

1) Maintenance to grounds/roads/car parks and parklands.
2) Supply /storage transportation of hazardous materials to the areas above.
3) Offloading/mixing/loading of hazardous materials to delivery vehicles, personal work equipment and land.
4) Cleaning of hazardous materials used in vehicles/personal work equipment and spillageis/surplus on land.
5) Drainage routes/interceptor tanks/settling ponds/overflow systems.
6) Building water systems/cooling towers/showers and fire mains.
7) Electrical/mechanical equipment replacement of oils and hydraulic fluids.
8) Limits for discharges of gases.

L) Final SHE Plan

Updated to include all amendments.

WORKED EXAMPLE 12.2

HANDOVER OF A PROCESS/PRODUCTION PLANT

The method of plant handover from the final erection through the initial checking and testing to takeover by the operator can be recorded by a system of certificates. The sequence of documents shown below is based on the Principal Contractor or Contractor installing and commissioning with a final handover to the Client or end user. The stage of handover can change according to the conditions of the contract but the principles of recording and controlling the commissioning procedures remain the same.

Issue Receipt	Certificate	Comments
By - Contractors To - Principal Contractor	Plant Erection Completion Certificate	Issued when plant is built and to include the defects and omissions list
By - Commissioning Team To - Commissioning Manager	Static Test Sheet	Issued when plant is manually operated
By - Commissioning Team To - Commissioning Manager	Safety Rule Implementation Certificate	Issued when plant is to be made live and used to control work or testing on or adjacent to the plant
By - Commissioning Manager To - Client's Site Manager or Agent	Record of initial operation certificate	Issued after an initial operation and to include the defects and omissions list
By - Client's Site Manager or Agent To - Operational Manager	Clearance for operation certificate	The operational Manager accepts responsibility for the plant subject to any defects and omissions.
By - Client's Project Manager To - Client	Internal taking over certificate	This notifies the Client of the contractual take over date and the start of the maintenance period
By - Client's Project Manager To - Client/End User	Final Clearance certificate	Issued one month before the expiry of the maintenance period and to list the outstanding defects and omissions.

CHAPTER 13

OPERATION, MAINTENANCE & FACILITIES MANAGEMENT

13.1   Introduction

This chapter highlights the activities within the total project management of the construction process that need to be addressed in order to provide the basis for SHE control during the operation, maintenance and facilities management of process plant, buildings and offices. It has been accepted that attention to SHE issues in design can not only provide safer construction but will result in more efficient operation, safer maintenance and facility management. In this chapter, the term 'facility' has been used to describe the building or process/production plant.

13.2   Summary of Key Issues

*   Buildings with complex systems for heating and ventilation require high levels of maintenance whereas plant with few automatic controls require high levels of operating personnel.

*   The consideration of stores holding of spare equipment.

*   The access to maintain and clean internal and external plant building services.

*   The elimination of manual handling.

*   Design of floor finish - traffic /process/special requirements/cleaning method.

*   Personal Protective Equipment.

*   Disabled workers.

*   Fire evacuation.

*   Design
    (reference *Human Factors in Industrial Safety*. Published by HMSO HSE Reference No: HS(G)48 and ISBN No. 0 11 885486 0).

Operational systems should be fail safe and must take into consideration human fallibility. The designer has to build in systems to minimise the effects of human failure. Often systems of control are installed for the economic considerations without a review of the resulting difficulty this may cause to the operator.

*   Analysis of the operator critical tasks and risks of failure.

*   Evaluation of decisions to be made between automatic and physical controls.

*   Consideration of emergency actions required and the display of process information.

*   Arrangement for maintenance access.

*   Provision of working environment for lighting , noise, and thermal considerations.

The design team need to take into consideration the mode of operation, maintenance of the facility which will require a risk assessment of hazards identified.

The mode of operation may require little operator action if for example continuous operation of the facility was required at a steady state. Whereas frequent start up and shut down or variable production rates may require constant changes in plant controls. The amount of automatic control will reduce the risk to operators but may require increased maintenance and consequently the increased risk to maintenance personnel must be considered by the designer. The primary hazard being access to the plant whilst in operation.

The maintenance criteria may be on a routine preventative basis or left to a breakdown/ replacement regime. If frequent access to plant controls is required then access can be permanently designed for the facility. If breakdown maintenance is accepted then equipment installed to assist fast turnaround is the designers consideration.

The maintenance criteria can also have an impact on stores location, access routes, amount of access available around the facility.

The facilities management requires the operator/client to specify the required parameters - minimal management with low numbers of staff available for the building and consequently control systems fully automated, simple design with internal and external of high durability and easily cleaned surfaces.

13.3   Forms of contract

Increasingly contracts for operating the facility are let to specialist companies (e.g. electrical supply), also contracts for maintenance are sub-contracted because of the need for short term high resource levels. Facilities management companies now offer to remove the responsibility from the client in order to allow the client to concentrate on its core business. The company taking responsibility for this work will now become a Principal Contractor.

13.4   Pre qualification Stage

Screening of potential contractors to confirm that they have the necessary expertise, experience and capability to undertake the project.

Used to prepare a list of contractors who may be invited to bid for a project.

Should identify those who are clearly unsuitable to undertake the work by identifying deficiencies in their organisation and administration arrangements which would suggest that they would be unable to undertake the SHE requirements of the project.

May be used for a one off project or to provide a pool of contractors who may be invited to submit bids for a series of contracts (i.e. may need to be updated from time to time).

Screening arrangements should include

- Questionnaire

- Evaluation of previous experience of contractor

- Assessment of contractor's general reputation within industry.

- Tender Evaluation

Evaluate and compare SHE aspects of bid responses

- SHE plans

- Key personnel

- Proposed sub-contractors

- Management / Method statements for project specific SHE issues

- Provision of costs for SHE activities

- Provision of SHE training

Review selection criteria against current project plan to ensure that assumptions used to define criteria are still valid.

Prequalification Checklist

To aid development of a contractor selection strategy the following checklist has been developed. The checklist is not exhaustive and particular attention should be paid to project specific SHE issues.

13.4.1   Management And Leadership

- Assess commitment and attitude of Principal Contractor's to project SHE objectives.

- Review Principal Contractor's SHE performance on previous contracts (where possible)

- SHE problems on other sites

- Review proposed management team's SHE experience

- CVs etc.

- Seek evidence that SHE objectives are given the appropriate priority compared with other management objectives, including :

    - General SHE objectives
    - Project specific SHE objectives
    - SHE training.

- Review quality of relationships with external SHE authorities.

- Pre-employment medicals - occupational health

13.4.2   Organisations and Rules

The response time of the organisation to breakdown, changes in operation, and changing requirements for the facility have to be seen to be effective to maintain an efficient and safe plant and high morale amongst personnel.

- Review Principal Contractor's organisational structure with specific reference to:

- Company organisation for general SHE including director responsible for SHE

- Company organisation for SHE

- Line responsibility for SHE

- Review actual rules issued to employees

- Review SHE consultation structures

- How does the Principal Contractor review/enforce compliance with SHE rules?

- Does the Principal Contractor review the need for specific SHE rules for each project?

- Does the Principal Contractor employ external SHE advisers?

- On what basis?

- Input into the project SHE

- Do jobs description and personnel specification define SHE responsibilities?

- Review training, competence and experience of Principal Contractor's SHE specialist and advisers

- Location and use of the SHE File and Health and Safety policy documentation and manuals

13.4.3   SHE Training

- Assess the adequacy of SHE training provided by the Principal Contractor to all levels in the organisation

- Review contents of Principal Contractor's induction course:

    - SHE policy, organisation and arrangements

    - Definition of responsibilities
    - Safe systems of work
    - SHE targets and performance criteria.

- Review content of internal and external SHE training courses used

- Does the Contractor provide special training in areas such as:

    - Operation of plant and machinery?

    - First Aid?

- Review ongoing and on the job SHE training procedures

- Training in emergency procedures

13.4.4   Control of on-site design changes

- Assess the adequacy of procedures for change controls

    Assuming the designer has addressed access for the operation and maintenance, the provision of built in work equipment and environmental issues. The primary method of risk reduction will be by working procedures.

        Working Procedures
        - Fire Safety
        - Housekeeping
        - Bomb Threat
        - First Aid
        - Eye Test

- Equipment-servicing, maintenance, repair and transport.
- Drainage
- Lighting
- Plant Rooms
- Floor Inspections
- Welfare Facilities

SHE Objectives
- Hazard identification
- Risk reduction requirement.

Additional Areas to address:

Cleaning - internal fabric, internal services systems (e.g. waste systems, air ducts), external fabric, external service system, (e.g. cooling towers).

Welfare Facilities for personnel - Changing and resting areas for ancilliary staff, in particular cleaning and catering staff, must be considered at the design stage. This will ensure that relevant legislation (e.g. food hygiene) is followed.

Manual Handling - elimination of manual handling or where essential use of personnel specifically trained - change culture from DIY to service personnel.

- Do the Principal Contractor's working procedures ensure that SHE objectives are met?

- Does the Principal Contractor systematically assess project SHE hazards?

- Provision of written method statements

- Provision and use of safe working systems such as:

  - Heavy lifting procedure
  - Permit to work procedures
  - Excavations
  - Working at height
  - Use and handling of Radioactive sources
  - Demolition
  - Steel erection
  - Lasers
  - Handling and use of hazardous substances.

- Procedures to advise statutory and regulatory authorities of "high risk" activities.

13.4.5   Procurement Controls

- What are the Principal Contractor's procedures for ensuring that the project SHE requirements are imposed on vendors?

13.4.6   Emergency Procedures

- Assess the Principal Contractor's emergency procedures

  - General competence of personnel

  - Understanding of required actions

- Assess the Contractor's procedures for dealing with emergency situations such as:

  - Excavation collapse

  - Localised fires

  - Means of escape

  - Site evacuation

  - Toxic gas escape

  - Fire / explosions

- What emergency first aid facilities does the Principal Contractor provide?

13.4.7   Planned Inspections

- What arrangements / procedures does the Principal Contractor have in place for SHE inspection and audit, including corrective actions?

- Review the Principal Contractor's arrangements to comply with statutory requirements for inspection, examination and notification of items such as:

  - Cranes, plant and equipment

  - Excavations

  - Scaffolds

- Review the Principal Contractor's "house keeping" arrangements

13.4.8   SHE Audits

- Policy

- Emergency Procedure

- Information induction training for employees

- Environmental Audit

- Does the Principal Contractor use a formal SHE auditing system?

- What are the details of the auditing system?

- How are the results of audits fed back and disseminated throughout the organisation?

Example of Environmental Audit

- Process - discharge limits

- COSHH

- Waste control

- Energy efficiency

- Noise

- Storage of hazardous substances

13.4.9 Incident/Accident Investigations

- What systems does the Principal Contractor have in place for Incident / Accident investigation and reporting?

- Who in the Principal Contractor's organisation has responsibility for such investigations?

- What are their competencies and have they been trained?

- How are the results from investigations communicated and followed up throughout the organisation?

  - Amendments to procedures

  - Implementation of recommendations

  - Does the Principal Contractor keep accident and incident statistics? Such as:

    - Accident frequency rates

    - Prohibition, improvement notices and prosecutions

    - Fatalities

    - Lost time due to injuries

    - Property damage and near misses.

- How long are these statistics kept for?

- How are the statistics used?

  - Formulation of SHE policy?

  - In forming SHE action plans?

13.4.10 Recruitment and Placement

- Review Principal Contractor's procedures for hiring and placement:

  - Are SHE factors used in selection criteria?

  - Are SHE factors used in employee performance appraisal?

- When evidence of lack of SHE competence exists, what actions are taken?

- How does the Principal Contractor ensure that adequate record keeping, certification, etc, is monitored for staff undertaking specialised trades?

13.4.11 Occupational Health

- What arrangements does the Principal Contractor have in place to provide a healthy workplace for its employees?

- What instruction/information is provided to employees on occupational health hazards?

- Does the Principal Contractor require employees to undertake regular medical examinations?

- Are medical examinations a part of the recruitment process?

- Does the Principal Contractor carry out reviews of work practices with a view to eliminating or reducing hazardous working conditions?

- What are the Principal Contractor's procedures for assessing project health risks prior to project execution?

13.4.12 Personal Protective Equipment (PPE)

- How does the Principal Contractor manage personal protective equipment?

  - Inventory management

  - Provision of PPE to employees

  - Instruction in use

  - Records of issue and training

  - Cleaning, maintenance and storage

- Do the Principal Contractor's project planning procedures recognise the provision of personal protective equipment?

13.4.13 Communications

- How are SHE requirements and expectations communicated to employees and their representatives

  - Formal issue

  - Notice boards

  - Safety bulletins etc

  - Via supervisors (toolbox talks etc)

- Do senior management communicate a commitment to SHE by their actions for example by visiting and walking the site?

- What role do the Principal Contractor's SHE professionals have in communicating SHE issues?

13.4.14 Meetings

- Does the Principal Contractor hold regular meetings on SHE matters?

  - Types of meeting

  - Frequency of meetings

- • Attendance

- • Senior Management involvement

- Safety committee

- Safety representatives

- Employees (Tool box talks)

- Content

- Records and minutes

13.4.15 Promotions

- How does the Principal Contractor promote acceptable SHE behaviour?

  - • Posters

  - • Notice boards

  - • Videos etc

- Are the Principal Contractor and contractors willing to be involved in site-wide co-ordination of SHE initiatives?

- What experience does the Principal Contractor have in SHE motivational schemes?

- How does the Principal Contractor react to SHE suggestions from employees?

13.4.16 Off the Job Safety

- What action does the Principal Contractor take to promote SHE issues outside the workplace?

13.5 Tender assessment/evaluation

Screening of tenderers to determine that they have the necessary competence i.e. skills and expertise to carry out the project in accordance with the SHE plan.

Confirmation that they have allocated sufficient resources and allowed sufficient time to complete the project in accordance with the project SHE plan.

Evaluate and compare SHE aspects of bids responses

- SHE plan

- Key personnel

- Proposed Contractors and Sub-contractors

- Method statements for specific SHE issues

- Provision of resources for SHE activities

- Provision of SHE training

Tender assessment/evaluation Check list

To aid development of a strategy for assessing the SHE aspects of contractor bids the following checklist has been developed. The checklist is not exhaustive and particular attention should be paid to project specific SHE issues.

13.5.1   SHE Plan

- Assess the procedures the Principal Contractor will adopt for developing and implementing the SHE plan.

- Determine whether the Principal Contractor has adequately addressed the risks identified in the plan and taken sufficient steps to control them.

- Determine whether the Principal Contractor has identified all the hazards arising from his operations and taken sufficient steps to control them.

- Assess the time allowed to complete the various stages of the project without risks to health and safety.

13.5.2   Management Systems

- The arrangements the Principal Contractor will put in place to actively manage SHE.

    - Project specific SHE policy

    - Provision of and access to specialist advice

    - Quality plans and programme

- Review proposed management teams SHE experience - CV's etc.

Co-operation with and co-ordination of other contractors activities

- What arrangements will the Principal Contractor have in place to ensure that his activities do not create a hazard to other employees and vice versa?

- How will the SHE performance of contractors and sub-contractors be assessed?

13.5.3   Involvement of employees

- How will SHE information be provided to employees?

- What arrangement will be made to seek the views of employees on SHE matters ?

- What training will be provided to employees?

13.5.4   Compliance with statutory requirements

- How will statutory requirements be complied with e.g.

    - Assessments of risk such as chemicals or noise

    - Accident reporting and investigation procedures.

    - Provision and use of personal protective equipment.

    - Welfare arrangements

13.5.5 Specific SHE initiatives

- Planned inspections

- Toolbox talks

- Safety promotions

WORKED EXAMPLE 13.1

FACILITIES MANAGEMENT FOR AN ADMINISTRATION BUILDING

SAFETY CHECK LIST

MONTHLY REPORT

FACILITIES MANAGEMENT FOR AN ADMINISTRATION BUILDING

ITEM	02-Jan	09-Jan	16-Jan	23-Jan	COMMENTS	ACTION BY	STATUS (O OR C)*
STATUTORY/SAFETY CHECKS							
ELECTRICAL TESTING							
WATER QUALITY							
EMERGENCY LIGHTING							
LIFTS (PASSENGER & HOIST)							
CRANES							
FIRE ALARM							
HALON EQUIPMENT							
HOSE REELS							
FIRE EXTINGUISHERS							
FUME CUPBOARDS							
PRESSURE VESSELS							
LADDERS							
HYDRAULIC TESTING							
WINDOW EYEBOLTS							
PROGRAMMED MAINTENANCE							
MONITORING							
PLANT ROOM EQUIPMENT							
GWB ELECTRODE BOILER							
YORK PLANT ENERGY PACK							
VENTILATION EQUIPMENT							
FUME CUPBOARDS							
AIR CONDITIONING SYSTEM							
AIR QUALITY MONITORING							
BUILDING							
INTERNAL DECORATION							
EXTERNAL DECORATION							
INTERNAL DOOR CLOSERS							
EXT'L SHUTTER DOORS							
ROOF							
LIFTS							
GROUNDS							
LANDSCAPE MTCE							
ROADS/PATHWAYS/HARD STANDING							
MISC							
CRANES							
LIFTING TACKLE							
CCTV EQUIP.							

* O = Ongoing, C = Completed

Courtesy of Trigon F.M.

CHAPTER 14

DECOMMISSIONING, DISMANTLING, DEMOLITION

14.1   Introduction

It is envisaged that Decommissioning and Dismantling are activities prior to Demolition or cessation of normal operations for the process/plant and, in the case of buildings, removal of occupancy. The organisation responsible for this work will now become a Principal Contractor.

With the implementation of the EEC Temporary or Mobile Construction Sites Directive which encompasses dismantling and demolition, but not explicitly decommissioning, a SHE File will be available to provide information for such work.

Decommissioning can result in accidents due to residual stored energy of components and incomplete drainage of hazardous substances.

Dismantling and demolition have both resulted in accidents due to premature collapse of building and structures.

14.1.1   Summary of Key Issues

- Client, Planning Supervisor and Principal Contractor formulate and agree SHE Plan.

- Client, Planning Supervisor and Principal Contractor agree monitoring system for implementation of SHE Plan.

- The management structure and communication systems are detailed with responsible personnel named and reporting routes.

- The safety rules, electrical, mechanical, radiological, hot work are defined and competent persons named to issue and receive permits.

- The training standards for the work are defined and on-going requirements are agreed, e.g. induction course.

- Working procedures are agreed for SHE control, e.g. emergency procedure, method statements.

- Method of checking performance to be used, e.g. collection of accident statistics, weekly SHE Inspections, Frequency of SHE Audits.

- Handover system, e.g. completion certificates, production of a SHE File for a future developer or occupier of the site.

14.1.2   Feasibility

The feasibility of decommissioning, dismantling and demolition must be assessed with respect to the selected option and final objective, i.e. can the SHE issues be managed? What are the resource requirements?

14.1.3   SHE Issues

Decommissioning can involve the removal of hazardous substances, the purging of systems, drainage systems with gas/liquid traps built in, removing plant containing fluids and gases under pressure, etc.

The following checklists can be used for these activities. In particular, attention should be given to waste disposal routes, the resultant environmental conditions of buildings and their surroundings and any remaining underground services.

It is essential that decommissioning activities feature in the project review (see Chapter 16) as this gives valuable feedback and provides a basis for future building work.

*   Decommissioning Check list

    Waste Control Routes
    Environmental Impact
    Ecological
    Residual Hazards
    Operational Safety Rules

*   Dismantling Check list

    Stability of Structure
    Noise
    Dust
    Vibration
    Residues from Previous Process
    Overload on Underground Services

*   Demolition Check list

    Stability of Structure
    Adjacent Properties
    Type of Structure
    Condition of Structure
    Health Hazards
    Residues from Previous Processes
    Waste Routes
    Noise
    Dust
    Vibration
    Previous or Present (Unauthorised) Occupancy

All possible sources of information regarding the building/site are required in order to assess a preferred option. The sources will indicate site surveys, reference to original planning drawings, reference to system drawings, existing operations and maintenance manuals, employees/ex-employees, local residents. Other sources can be Government Departments, e.g. Ministry of Defence.

14.2   Pre-Tender SHE Evaluation

Preparation of SHE Plan for inclusion in tender specification to include:

Timescale for completion
Existing environment
Existing drawings
Planning restrictions:
Traffic movements

Noise limits
Vibration limits
Hazard identification, to include:
*   known health hazards,
*   materials,
*   existing services,
*   fragile materials,
*   ground conditions.

Risk assessment of identified hazards to prioritise specific problems for reducing the risk or precautions that are required to be followed for managing risks.

The objective of the hazard identification risk process could be to completely eliminate the hazard, i.e. remove the requirement to manage the risk through site procedures. The reason for complete elimination would be to ensure the site was left with any residual hazards as any potential delay in developing the site would increase the risk of persons coming into contact with remaining hazards.

The disconnection of the system, dissipation of residual energy and handover of the area for demolition, dismantling, decommissioning must be clearly recorded and this information shown on the site drawings of terminal points.

It is often an advantage to complete a SHE Appraisal of demolition companies, both their company SHE procedures and site operations. This will provide assurance of the competence of the company to complete the work safely.

14.3   Enquiry Controls

The design methods of dismantling, decommissioning and demolition must be recorded with respect to the circulation list, revision number, date of issue, engineers responsible and comments received. All subsequent changes to engineering information contained in the SHE plan, method statement which alters the degree of risk must be recorded. An efficient system of ensuring the site team are working to the latest information must be set up and available during safety audits.

14.4   Tender Evaluation

The evaluation of tenders should ensure that resources are committed to manage SHE issues, the competence of such resources, the programme is capable of achieving the time scale with progressive labour build-up to match sequential work. The tenderer should be able to supply information on communication, training and SHE inspection methods which are established practices within the company. The accident statistics record for previous work should be compared with the SHE national figures.

Any outstanding issues from the evaluation can be resolved by using a supplementary questions systems. This enables the tenderers to explain fully their SHE controls.

14.5   Checklist

14.5.1   Management and Leadership

In order to manage the SHE requirements, a decision has to be taken on contract strategy which provides the basic structure for the organisation, e.g. Turnkey Contract/Multi Contracts managed by the client. For all types of contract, the major consideration is the risks to existing buildings and plant which may be still in use or operational, or to risks to the general public, i.e. surrounding buildings and infrastructure.

The management structure should define the communication route from the person responsible for the company health and safety policy through to the site operative. The methods of implementing this policy, i.e. planning, risk assessment, design review process, site rules/procedures, SHE meetings, SHE inspections and audits. The persons responsible for delivering the implementation of the policy and the method of recording and actioning such control.

The reduction in ratio of numbers of operatives to supervisor has been shown to reduce accidents, e.g. 1:5.

14.5.2   Organisation and Rules

With this type of work all operatives have to understand the sequence of decommissioning, dismantling and demolition, therefore method statements, operational procedures, zoning arrangements and terminal points have to be documented. The work areas which can be dispersed over large sites require teams allocated with respective supervisors.

The rules for the work in particular permit systems for decommissioning and access to confined spaces require to be defined.

14.5.3   SHE Training

Managers, supervisors and operatives have to be provided with the health and safety plan. The plan should permit feedback to change the plan, e.g. sequence of work. The plan should consist of method statements/operational procedures, which should be detailed to operatives, and a record retained of information provided by the employer.

The individual task requirements should be assessed by the employer and additional/specific training provided to ensure manager/supervisor/operative competence.

The operations of permit systems require assessments of competence for persons compiling permits and applying isolations to persons responsible for receiving permits and carrying out work.

14.5.4   Working Procedures

The Client, Planning Supervisor and Principal Contractor will need to define the boundaries of control for the site, i.e. where the client requires to retain the SHE Control. Often systems cross the control boundaries and it is essential to define the isolation points, method of requesting such isolations, responsibilities for ensuring isolations are safe.

The procedures may require the Client, Planning Supervisor and Principal Contractor input to ensure SHE control.

The number of procedures required will depend on the identified hazards and risk rating.

The detailed method of working which will include sequence, access, PPE and technical requirements will be defined in a method statement. The priority for producing a method statement is as the result of the identified high risk activities.

The monitoring of the implementation of the method statements, working procedures, SHE Plan will require a defined procedure and reporting system.

- Planned Inspections
- Reviews and Audits
- Accident/Incident Investigation
- Recruitment and Placement

14.5.5 Emergency Procedures

The major high risk activity is explosive demolition or weakening/toppling of large structures. The emergency procedure must be developed in the form of a contingency plan for the "one off" situations. (See Worked Example 14.1)

The Demolition Team may include Client, Planning Supervisor, Principal Contractor and specialist contractors depending upon the complexity of the project.

- The Demolition Team must demonstrate that emergency procedures have been developed and are in place prior to commencement of construction activities, including the necessary interface with emergency services (both internal and external).

- The emergency procedures should be published and distributed to all parties, including outside bodies where appropriate, prior to site activities .

- The Demolition Team is to ensure that all staff are given adequate training in emergency procedures. Where appropriate an emergency co-ordinator should be appointed with suitable responsibilities and authority.

- Emergency procedures must be rehearsed regularly.

- Alarms and systems must be tested regularly.

- Emergency equipment and plant should be regularly inspected and maintained.

- Ensure liaison with outside emergency services, hospitals and doctors.

- Special meetings - these are often required where explosive demolition takes place and are essential to agree and inform the public, local authorities and statutory authorities of SHE plans and control measures.

14.5.6 Planned Inspections

- The SHE inspections are to ensure continued and satisfactory SHE performance.

- Planned and systematic SHE inspections are to be carried out using trained personnel. Frequency of the inspections will recognise the nature of the construction activities, the hazards present and the performance on the site.

- The Demolition Team's SHE management systems shall describe corrective actions required in the event of non compliance with SHE procedures.

- The Demolition Team will ensure that statutory examinations, inspections and notifications for items such as plant, equipment, excavations, medical facilities, etc., are carried out at the required intervals.

- Records, certificates and registers are to be kept, where appropriate, in a central location. They are to be monitored regularly to ensure that they comply with SHE and regulatory requirements.

14.5.7 SHE Audits

- The Team shall ensure that SHE monitoring by the team forms a regular part of site SHE activities.

- The Demolition Team shall periodically audit the SHE management systems and procedures to ensure the goals of the construction SHE plan are being achieved. Where necessary corrective actions are to be detailed and implemented.

14.5.8 Incident / Accident Investigations

- The Demolition Team, through the SHE management systems and procedures, shall ensure that all accidents and incidents are reported and investigated. The incident/accident investigation procedures should:

  - Comply with appropriate statutory reporting requirements
  - Be carried out by competent, trained staff
  - Follow agreed methods and procedures
  - Require senior management attention and action
  - Provide feedback of root causes and allow learning
  - Allow the compilation of suitable statistics
  - Determine trends and detail corrective actions.

- Recommendations from accident investigations should be implemented to an agreed schedule. Safety procedures, practices and training should be modified to prevent recurrence of incidents.

- Near miss incidents should be investigated and communicated as learning events.

14.5.9 Recruitment and Placement

- The Demolition Team should arrange the necessary induction training and instruction for all new employees and transfers.

- The Demolition Team's recruitment practice should recognise SHE criteria in the screening and selection of employees.

- Site personnel who carry out specialised tasks such as crane driving, banksman, scaffolding, etc., must be properly trained and their competency regularly monitored.

14.5.10 Occupational Health

- The Demolition Team should ensure that employees undergo pre-employment and regular medical examinations where appropriate.

- The Demolition Team should carry out reviews of work practices to eliminate or reduce hazardous conditions.

- The Demolition Team is to ensure that hazardous substances are identified, assessments made and procedures for use are prepared before work commences.

Two of the major health issues concern asbestos and lead, and there are extreme precautions required for working with both substances defined in legislation. Contractors employing operatives should ensure that preliminary health screening is carried out to provide baseline data and acceptable levels.

14.5.11 Personal Protective Equipment (PPE)

- The Demolition Team must demonstrate adequate management systems for the provision and use of personal protective equipment. Items that need to be identified include:

  - Procedures for identifying PPE requirements for the project

- Employee instruction in use, storage and maintenance

- Recording issue and use of equipment

- Satisfactory inventory management systems for PPE.

- Extensive use of breathing apparatus occurs during this type of work, therefore reliable records and checks of equipment must be available on site.

14.5.12   Communications

- The Demolition Team are to ensure effective communication of SHE procedures and policies within the team and to all employees. Specific items that should be identified include:

  - Role of supervisors and health and safety officers

  - Method of communication (Tool-box talks etc.)

  - Feedback from employees.

- This type of work often has an effect on the public environment and consequently local authorities should be kept informed of the possible results, e.g. noise, vibration, dust, air pressure and transport of waste.

14.5.13   Meetings

- The Demolition Team should hold planned and informal group meetings on a regular basis. Participants should include managers, supervisors and staff.

- Regular on-site project SHE meetings with all parties attending (client, contractors, sub-contractors teams, safety advisers and, where appropriate, appointed trade union representatives) should be convened.

- A suitable agenda should be developed and circulated prior to this meeting.

- Planned meetings should be minuted with actions summarised and implemented and progress monitored.

14.5.14   Promotion

- Safe behaviour and a proactive SHE culture should be promoted throughout the construction phase using:

  - Management/leadership
  - Enforcement of SHE procedures
  - Tool box talks
  - Posters
  - Displays
  - Safety Representatives and employee participation
  - Videos
  - Competitions
  - Notice boards displaying SHE statistics
  - Information handouts
  - Promotional campaigns (using actual site incidents as source material)
  - Involvement of SHE professionals
  - Employee participation in the promotion of the SHE culture.

14.5.15   Off the Job Safety

- Encourage SHE awareness outside of the work place, for the benefit of both employee and employer.

- As part of the SHE programme highlight off-the-job risks and foster a positive attitude towards high safety standards and make safety awareness a matter of habit.

- It is important to emphasise the dangers of additional work outside which could affect health surveillance, e.g. lead in blood reading.

WORKED EXAMPLE 14.1

CONTINGENCY PLAN FOR DEMOLITION OF REINFORCED CONCRETE CHIMNEYS

HAZARD/RISK

1.1   There could be three main scenarios arising from this type of operation, a misfire (total or partial), a partial collapse leaving an unstable structure, or a total collapse but in a unpredicted direction.

1.2   Any misfire situation would be assessed by the explosive engineers representative, following a detailed inspection of the structure. A mutually acceptable course of action will then be agreed between all site parties. Any courses of action will be put in writing prior to commencement.

1.3   With regard to a partial collapse leaving a dangerous structure, once again this situation will be dependent on the particular circumstances at the time. As an example, it may require further preweakening followed by further detonation of explosives or possibly some form of remote mechanical demolition may be required. Again, this will be agreed in writing and the major existing demolition plant currently on site would be utilised unless a specific piece needed to be brought in, in which case the site would be adequately secured until the next move could be carried out. In an event of this nature, an accurate assessment of the stability of the remaining structure would need to be carried out. Once again, this would comprise detailed discussions and agreement with the relevant site personnel and the course of action put in writing.

1.4   Should the structures fall in a totally unpredicted direction, this would not put any lives at risk because of the size of the exclusion zone. The major problem here would be if the chimneys fell onto the adjacent buildings which could lead to structural problems, although once again this would need to be assessed and a suitable course of action undertaken, again in writing.

1.5   Adequate plant and equipment will be on site to deal with most situations.

1.6   Emergency services will already be present on site so that any other possible emergency problems can be dealt with.

1.7   While all discussions are taking place to establish the course of action, following any emergency situation, the flagmen will remain in position and the site secured until new proposals are submitted.

1.8   Demolition Company operatives will be available on site to pick up and collect any small particles that may have landed on surrounding properties, although in this particular instance this is highly unlikely.

1.9   .... will be the responsible officer for the whole operation on the day although also on site will be senior personnel from both Demolition Company and Explosives Company.

SEQUENCE OF EVENTS FOR THE DEMOLITION OF THE CHIMNEYS

DEMOLITION OF 2 NO. REINFORCED CONCRETE CHIMNEYS

Sequence of the Day of Felling

8.30 am   Head count of all staff and Demolition Company staff remaining on the site during the operation.

Itemise list of personnel entering and leaving the site to keep a tally on the overall numbers.

8.45 am   Secure demolition area.

8.50 am   Clear site of all non-essential personnel.

9.00 am   Check site to ensure all staff not associated with the controlled demolition of the chimneys are removed.

9.10 am   Establish exclusion zone.

Place flagmen (White Suits/Blue Helmets/Red Flags/Radios).

9.30 am   Radio Check.

9.45 am   Radio Check.

9.50 am   Warning Siren - 30 seconds continuous.

9.59 am + 30 seconds   Warning shot.

10.00 am   Detonation.

10.05 am   Explosive Engineer to inspect debris and structure.

10.10 am (approx.)   All Clear Siren - 30 seconds intermittent.

No-one must move towards the demolition area until the All Clear has sounded.

Disband Flagmen.

CHAPTER 15

PROJECT SHE AUDIT

15.1 Introduction

This book has attempted to provide a Total Project Management approach to the management of Safety, Health and the Environment.

In this chapter we examine ways in which companies can verify or audit how we have performed at each stage in the project cycle. At the end of the audit process we should be left with a 'snapshot' of the projects strengths and weaknesses and with a clear indication where future actions are required.

The SHE audit measures performance. The most obvious measure at the end of a project is the number of accidents that have occurred. This information will be useful in planning for the future and setting new standards. Unfortunately this will be of little comfort to those who may have received an injury during the life of the project.

Auditing, however, is a pro-active management technique and should provide a powerful insight into identifying precisely where improvements are necessary and thereby enable preventative actions to be taken where necessary.

15.1.1 Why do we audit SHE?

- to measure safety performance

- to provide an indication of safety priorities

- to pinpoint weaknesses

- to identify training needs

- to assess workforce commitment/apathy

- to ensure responsibilities are understood

By examining these and other aspects of our SHE management systems, the SHE audit provides us with a means of making improvements to existing standards, hopefully before an accident or incident occurs.

SHE auditing provides the method of monitoring and controlling SHE activities and procedures throughout the life of the project. It is a mechanism for providing feedback on how well the project is meeting its SHE objectives and in a wider sense, how well the company is achieving the corporate goals of the Safety, Health & Environment Policy.

15.1.2 What do we audit?

In this respect the SHE audit should consider:

- objectives

- organisation

- responsibilities, levels of authority, delegated powers

- plans and policy reviews

- programmes and practices.

15.2   Audits and Inspections

SHE auditing is often used to describe an activity which is really an inspection of a specific aspect of SHE activity. Auditing is a much broader process which would happen much less frequently in the project cycle than SHE inspections, which could take place daily on a large complex project.

15.2.1   SHE Audits

Provide a more comprehensive and formal assessment of compliance with SHE procedures and plans.

These audits should be carried out at key points during the project life cycle as illustrated in Figure 15.1

The frequency and scope of SHE audits during the construction phase should be highlighted in the SHE Plan and explicitly recognised in the contract documentation.

15.2.2   SHE Inspections

Provide the day to day or week to week means of checking compliance with project SHE requirements. This could include a wide range of specific issues which affect Safety, Health & the Environment. These are normally contained within a regular programme of SHE inspection, for example:

- Safety documentation

- Permits

- She training and induction

- Safe access

- Ladders, steps and lightweight stagings

- Tubular scaffolds

- Excavations

- Roofwork

- Falsework

This list is by no means exhaustive. Projects should develop their own listings in line with their own specific hazards and safety requirements.

The results from all audits and inspections must be fed back to the relevant parties as soon as possible to allow corrective actions to be instigated.

Figure 15.1 Project Stages

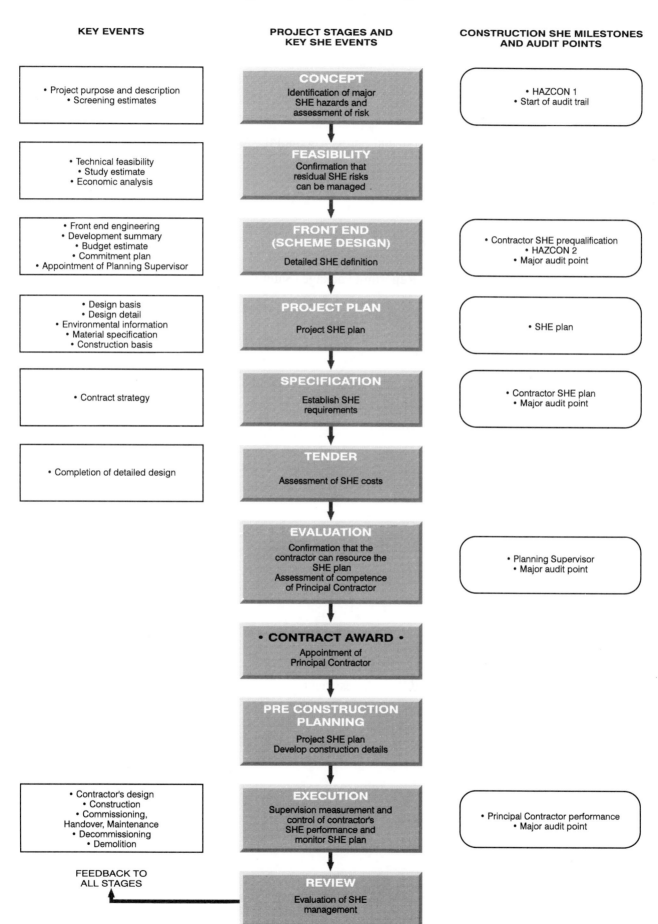

A number of proprietary audit systems exist that may be appropriate for project SHE auditing, including:

- International Safety Rating System (ISRS)

- British Safety Council System

- Construction Chase (Health and Safety Technology Management Ltd, Aston University)

- Coursafe (Courtaulds)

- DuPont Safety Services

- Safety and Health Audit Reporting Package (Safety and Reliability Ltd)

- ROSPA System

15.3 SHE Audit Checklist

The following checklist describes activities and procedures that should be audited during the life time of the project. The checklist can be developed for use as the project review tool (see chapter 16).

15.3.1 SHE Plan

- Policy

- Applicable legislation

- Standards

- Procedures

- Rules

- Hazard identification and Risk Assessment

- Health Medical and Welfare

- Auditing programme

- Environmental issues

- Use of contractors and sub-contractors

15.3.2 Management and Supervision

- SHE Organisation

- Communication of SHE plan

- Management of the work place

- Management of tasks and operations

- SHE performance

- Emergency response procedures

15.3.3 Training (General and Specialised)

- Induction programmes

- SHE promotion and awareness

- SHE training

- SHE professionals

15.3.4 Plant Equipment and Maintenance

- SHE Equipment

- SHE inspection (plant and equipment)

- Hygiene and Housekeeping

- Personal Protective Equipment

15.3.5 Incident / Accident Reporting

- Incident / Accident investigation

- Data collection and statistics

WORKED EXAMPLE 15.1

PROJECT SHE AUDIT

PARTIES INVOLVED

Ref No	Question	Y	N	N/A	Comments
	Did the type of contractual arrangement provide an acceptable level of SHE throughout the project?				
	Did professional advisers meet the SHE objectives of the project?				
	Did the Planning Supervisor control SHE pre-site?				
	Did the designers achieve the design for SHE?				
	Did the Principal Contractor control SHE on site?				
	Did the Contractors and Sub-contractors achieve the SHE objectives of the project?				
	Were the management structures for control of SHE clearly shown by the Client, Planning Supervisor and Contractor?				
	Was a safety co-ordinator appointed for each stage of the project?				
	Were the SHE lessons of the project fed back to all interested parties?				

Continued/....

PROJECT SHE AUDIT (Contd)

SHE POLICY

Ref No	Question	Y	N	N/A	Comments
	Was the company SHE policy statement and Project Notification Form displayed in the Main office/site Office/Site Mess Room?				
	Was a local safety statement based upon the Company Policy displayed in the Main office/site office/site mess room?				
	Were employees informed of the contents of the company policy/local statement/SHE Plan?				
	Were the employees informed of their responsibilities within the policy/local statement/ SHE Plan?				
	Was there a method of improving/feedback changes to the policy /local statement/SHE Plan?				
	Were Contractors and Sub-contractors safety policies displayed?				
	Were the targets for SHE described in the policy/local statement/SHE Plan achieved?				
	Did managers take positive action to implement the policy eg through site safety inspections?				
	Was safety management performance included in the staff appraisal?				
	Were the Client's SHE objectives discussed with the Planning Supervisor and Principal Contractor?				
	Were the SHE objectives defined for the relevant responsible personnel?				
	Were the SHE objectives reported on by the relevant responsible personnel?				

Continued/....

PROJECT SHE AUDIT (Contd)

INITIAL CONCEPT/PROJECT OBJECTIVES

Ref No	Question	Y	N	N/A	Comments
	Were SHE objectives defined for the Project?				
	Did the Client and Planning Supervisor provide SHE information at this stage?				
	Were SHE standards used as a basis?				
	Was there an overall structure for disseminating SHE standards?				
	Was there compliance with the SHE standards?				
	Was staffing allocated to manage SHE requirements?				
	Was sufficient time allowed for SHE?				
	Was SHE management performance included in the staff appraisal?				
	Were hazard identifications and risk assessments carried out?				
	Were actions taken from the results of risk assessments?				

Continued/....

PROJECT SHE AUDIT (Contd)

DESIGN

Ref No	Question	Y	N	N/A	Comments
	Were the SHE requirements clearly defined by the Client and Planning Supervisor?				
	Were critical tasks defined by the Client and Planning Supervisor?				
	Were the Principal Contractors informed of the SHE requirements of the design and specifications?				
	Were the Contractors and Sub-contractors informed of their SHE responsibilities within the design?				
	Was there a method of improving/feedback changes to the SHE design?				
	Were specialists involved in design reviews?				
	Did the Planning Supervisor take positive action to check the design for SHE contents?				
	Was SHE design management performance included in the staff appraisal?				
	Was there a formal SHE review of design changes?				
	Did the design include a formal risk assessment?				
	Did the design result in SHE problems?				

SHE PLAN

Ref No.	Question	Y	N	N/A	Comments
	Was the SHE Plan produced?				
	Were responsibilities clearly defined in the SHE Plan?				
	Did the SHE Plan clearly identify the client's requirements?				
	Was the SHE Plan updated throughout the project?				
	Was the SHE Plan included in the tender evaluation?				
	Did the SHE Plan improve safety performance?				
	Were adequate resources allowed for the SHE Plan?				

Did the Planning Supervisor co-ordinate all the inputs to the SHE Plan?

SHE COSTS & BENEFITS

Ref No	Question	Y	N	N/A	Comments

Was sufficient time and money allocated to the project for SHE requirements?

Were additional funds made available during the project?

Did employees receive all the personal protective equipment costed for the project?

Was safety performance linked to costs?

Did purchasing specifications contain SHE requirements?

Did the project result in additional SHE costs?

Were there cost benefits in the control of SHE?

Was there an expectations gap between:

  • Client and Principal Contractors?

  • Principal Contractor and Contractors/Sub-contractors?

Was site productivity improved on the project when compared to typical projects/contracts?

Was lost time due to accidents reduced when compared to typical projects/contracts?

Was morale increased when compared to typical projects/contracts?

Was absenteeism reduced on this project when compared to typical projects/contracts?

Continued/....

PROJECT SHE AUDT (Contd)

CONTRACTUAL ARRANGEMENTS

Ref No	Question	Y	N	N/A	Comments
	Did the contract specification between Client and Principal Contractor result in meeting all the SHE objectives for the project?				
	Did the contracts between the Principal Contractor and the Contractors/ Sub-contractors provide the SHE objectives for the project?				
	Were the training requirements for the project achieved?				
	Were the resources requested in the contract provided to meet SHE objectives?				
	Was there a method of measuring safety performance?				

ASSESSMENT OF COMPETENCE AND RESOURCES

Ref No	Question	Y	N	N/A	Comments
	Did the selection process provide the Contractors with the required SHE commitments?				
	Did the Principal Contractor's selection process provide Sub-contractors with the required SHE commitment?				
	Did the Contractor/Sub-contractor accident frequency/incidence rates improve during the project?				
	Did the Principal Contractor's safety assessment questionnaire provide all the SHE information of the Contractor/Sub-contractors?				
	Did the selection process adequately determine the competence and resrouces of the Principal Contractor?				
	Did the Principal Contractor adequately identify hazards and control risks arising during the project?				
	Did the Principal Contractor's site management effectively implement the SHE policy during the construction phase?				
	Was there sufficient communication and co-ordination between the various contractors (and the Principal Contractor) to ensure proper management of SHE issues?				

Continued/....

PROJECT SHE AUDIT (Contd)

PRE-CONSTRUCTION/CONSTRUCTION PLANNING

Ref No	Question	Y	N	N/A	Comments
	Was the SHE plan in place at this stage?				
	Did the project planners include SHE information in the programme?				
	Were the appointments of SHE professional advisors correct for the project?				
	Were method statements produced for all identified activities?				
	Were SHE requirements included in the method statements?				
	Did the relevant people in the project team comment on the method statements?				
	Did the time allowed for safety work prove to be adequate?				
	Were the arrangements for site e.g. procedures etc. set up in time for the work to start on site?				
	Did the site layout plan enable SHE requirements to be met?				
	Was the information regarding the SHE Plan communicated to all persons working on the project?				
	Was a SHE action plan produced?				
	Did the SHE action plan work?				
	Did the emergency procedures meet the requirements of the project?				
	Did the feedback arrangements work in providing the planners with SHE information?				
	Did the audit programme provide the feedback for improving the SHE of the project?				
	Was risk assessment adequate and effective?				

Continued/....

PROJECT SHE AUDIT (Contd)

CONSTRUCTION

Ref No	Question	Y	N	N/A	Comments
	Were the SHE objectives communicated to the site?				
	Was the induction course comprehensive enough for the project?				
	Were the SHE training requirements implemented on site?				
	Did the Principal Contractor inform Contractors and Sub-contractors of their SHE responsibilities?				
	Were the employees informed of their responsibilities within the policy/local statement/SHE Plan?				
	Was there a method improving/feedback changes to the policy/local statement/SHE Plan?				
	Was there a method of improving/feedback changes to the method statements?				
	Have the targets for SHE described in the policy/local statement/SHE Plan been achieved?				
	Did managers take positive action to implement the policy e.g. through site safety inspections?				
	Was SHE management performance included in the staff appraisal?				
	Did co-ordination of SHE requirements occur between Principal Contractors/Contractors/Sub-contractors work?				
	Were records kept of the SHE inspections on site?				
	Were accident/investigation reports produced for all such incidents?				
	Did the employees conform to the method statements?				
	Were emergency plans rehearsed during the construction?				
	Were health controls adequate for the work?				
	Was general promotion of SHE carried out on the site?				
	Were systematic inspections carried out during this phase?				
	Were audits carried out for specific work practices on site?				

Continued/....

PROJECT SHE AUDIT (Contd)

CONSTRUCTION (contd)

Ref No	Question	Y	N	N/A	Comments
	Did a follow-up audit ensure that remedial actions had been completed?				
	Was the Principal Contractor's performance regularly reviewed?				
	Was feedback on safety performance/audits given to employees, supervisors, managers?				
	Did the phase result in SHE problems?				

PRE-COMMISSIONING AND COMMISSIONING

Ref No	Question	Y	N	N/A	Comments
	Was the SHE Plan updated for Commissioning?				
	Were the commissioning team members assigned areas of SHE responsibilities?				
	Did the commissioning certificates clearly define the limitations of the plant system?				
	Was an assessment of the hazards carried out?				
	Was documentation completed satisfactorily?				
	Were the team trained with respect to the emergency procedure?				
	Was there remedial actions of the SHE reports implemented				
	Did managers take positive action to implement the policy e.g. through site safety inspections?				
	Was safety management performance included in the staff appraisal?				
	Did the commissioning result in SHE problems?				

Continued/....

PROJECT SHE AUDIT (Contd)

HANDOVER

Ref No	Question	Y	N	N/A	Comments
	Did the Client or end user agree that all SHE information had been supplied in the SHE File?				
	Was all the design criteria included in the SHE File?				
	Was all the SHE training specified in the SHE File?				
	Were all employees informed of the contents of the plant handover documentation?				
	Were all the employees informed of their responsibilities within the plant handover system?				
	Did the Commissioning Team carry out training on the use of the plant handover system?				
	Did the Commissioning Team define the limitations of the plant systems?				
	Was the plant identified clearly?				
	Did the operating/instructions require modification?				
	Did the maintenance instructions require modification?				

OPERATION MAINTENANCE AND FACILITIES MANAGEMENT

Ref No.	Question	Y	N	N/A	Comments
	Did the SHE File contain the O&M and FM information?				
	Did the client agree to the contents of the SHE File?				
	Did the Design Team include consideration of the operation and maintenance of the facility?				
	Was hazardous materials documentation adequate?				
	Were welfare facilities adequately designed?				
	Did the O&M and FM result in SHE problems?				

Continued/....

PROJECT SHE AUDIT (Contd)

DE-COMMISSIONING, DISMANTLING AND DEMOLITION

Ref No.	Question	Y	N	N/A	Comments
	Were the SHE objectives communicated to the site?				
	Was the induction course comprehensive enough for the project?				
	Were the SHE training requirements implemented on site?				
	Did the Principal Contractor inform Contractors and Sub-contractors of their SHE responsibilities?				
	Were the employees informed of their responsibilities within the policy/local statement/ SHE Plan?				
	Was there a method improving/feedback changes to the policy/local statement/SHE Plan?				
	Was there a method of improving/feedback changes to the method statements?				
	Have the targets for SHE described in the policy/local statement/SHE Plan been achieved?				
	Did managers take positive action to implement the policy e.g. through site safety inspections?				
	Was SHE management performance included in the staff appraisal?				
	Did co-ordination of SHE requirements occur between Principal Contractors/contractors/sub-contractors work?				
	Were records kept of the SHE inspections on site?				
	Were accident/investigation reports produced for all such incidents?				
	Did the employees conform to the method statements?				
	Were emergency plans rehearsed during the construction?				
	Were health controls adequate for the work?				
	Was general promotion of SHE carried out on the site?				
	Were systematic inspections carried out during this phase?				

Continued/....

PROJECT SHE AUDIT (Contd)

DE-COMMISSIONING, DISMANTLING AND DEMOLITION (CONTD)

Ref No.	Question	Y	N	N/A	Comments

Did a follow-up audit ensure that remedial actions had been completed?

Was the Principal Contractor's performance regularly reviewed?

Was feedback on safety performance/audits given to employees, supervisors, managers?

Did the phase result in SHE problems?

Was the Contingency Plan adequate for high risk activities?

CHAPTER 16

PROJECT REVIEWS

16.1   Introduction

Project reviews are **critical** to the successful development of SHE policy, plan, file and procedures.

This chapter describes a methodology for successfully completing the review at the end of a project.

Review and feedback should be continuous throughout the project life cycle. The purpose of the project review is to tie together the project team's experience and learning and provide feedback to this and future projects.

The methodology developed in this chapter should allow all parties involved in the project to answer the questions:

> "How effective was the SHE plan? What worked and what didn't work? What should be kept and what should be changed?"

16.2   Project Review

The review method described below allows project SHE formation to be viewed in the historical context of the project and provides pointers for future SHE development.

16.2.1   Review Methodology

- Review Design risk assessment results and compare with construction problems.

- Review Audit database

- Analysis of all accident/near misses/frequency/incidence rates

- Assess the effectiveness of the SHE plan
  - Identify issues not anticipated in the plan
  - Determine how these issues were resolved
  - What are the implications for future projects?
  - Integrate learning into revised plan

- Highlight positive aspects of plan that were successful and should be used in the future.

- Identify areas of the SHE plan that were less successful
  - Why were these areas less successful?
  - What can be done to improve these areas?
  - Develop and implement plan revisions

- Analyse SHE performance of all parties involved in the project
  - What factors determined performance?
  - What needs to be done to improve performance?
  - Discuss findings
  - Feedback experience and learning
  - Review performance of Planning Supervisor and Principal Contractor
  - Review performance of contractors and sub-contractors
  - Review pre-qualification parameters and amend database

- Feedback experience and learning throughout the project team and their respective organisations.

16.2.2 Checklist

Chapters 1 - 3   Are involved with the initial framework of safety for the project and should be the remit of the company for whom the project is being undertaken.

- Impact on company policy

- Impact on company procedures

- Impact on project feasibility

Chapters 4 - 9   These form the basis for the production of a SHE plan, the implication on SHE costs, the contractors ability and method of SHE implementation.

Chapters 10 - 15   These detail and implement the SHE plan and will result in a record of the safety performance of the Client/Planning Supervisor/Principal Contractor/Contractor/Sub-contractor.

It should contain an analysis of all accident/near misses/ frequency/ incidence rates.

16.2.3 Report

In order to obtain an agreed conclusion between the responsible parties for each section it is recommended that the review is conducted by an independent chairman. It is essential to concentrate on the SHE methods used and not the personalities involved.

In order to obtain the maximum benefit for all participants in future projects the report should be circulated to designers, client project teams, contractors and sub-contractors.

LEGISLATION

EUROPEAN DIRECTIVES

Available in the Official Journal - Legislation series (OJ L) from HMSO, London.

67/548/EEC	Directive on the approximation of laws, regulations and administration provisions relating to the classification, packaging and labelling of dangerous substances (Dangerous substances Directive) OJ L196, 16.8.67
73/23/EEC	Directive on harmonisation of laws of Member States relating to electrical equipment designed for use with certain voltage limits OJ L77, 26.3.73
80/1107/EEC	Directive on the protection of workers from the risks related to exposure to chemical, physical and biological agents at work. OJ L327, 3.12.80
82/501/EEC	Directive on major accidents hazards of certain industrial activities OJ L230, 5.8.82
83/477/EEC	Directive on the protection of workers from the risks related to exposure to asbestos at work OJ L263, 24.9.83
86/188/EEC	Directive on the protection of workers from the risks related to exposure to noise at work OJ L137, 24.5.86
89/106/EEC	Directive on the approximation of laws, regulations and administrative provisions of the Member States relating to construction products (Construction Products Directive) OJ L40, 11.2.89
89/336/EEC	Council Directive of 3.5.89 on the approximation of the laws of the Member States relating to electromagnetic compatibility (Electromagnetic compatibility 'EMC' Directive) OJ L139, 23.5.89
89/391/EEC	Directive of the introduction of measures to encourage improvements in the safety and health of workers at work (Framework Directive) OJ L183, 29.6.89
89/392/EEC (91/368/EEC)	Directive on the approximation of the laws of the Member States relating to machinery, as amended (Machinery Directive) OJ L183, 29.6.89: OJ L198, 22.7.91
89/654/EEC	Directive concerning the minimum safety and health requirements for the workplace (Workplace Directive) OJ L393, 30.12.89
89/655/EEC	Directive concerning the minimum safety and health requirements for the use of work equipment by workers at work (Use of work equipment Directive) OJ L393, 30.12.89

89/656/EEC	Directive on the minimum health and safety requirements for the use by workers of personal protective equipment at the workplace (Personal protective equipment Directive) OJ L393, 30.12.89
89/686/EEC	Directive on the approximation of the laws of EC Member States relating to personal protective equipment (Personal protective equipment 'PPE' Directive) OJ L 399, 30.12.89
90/269/EEC	Directive on the minimum health and safety requirements for the manual handling of loads where there is a risk particularly of back injury to workers (Manual handling of loads Directive) OJ L156, 21.6.90
90/270/EEC	Directive on the minimum safety and health requirements for work with display screen equipment (Display screen equipment 'VDU' Directive) OJ L156, 21.6.90
90/394/EEC	Directive on the protection of workers from the risks related to exposure to carcinogens at work (Carcinogens Directive) OJ L196, 26.7.90
90/396/EEC	Directive on the approximation of the laws of Member States relating to appliances burning gaseous fuels OJ L196, 26.7.90
92/57/EEC	Directive concerning temporary and mobile construction sites. (The basis of the UK CDM Regulations 1994) OJ L245/6, 26.8.92

EUROPEAN MEMBER STATE LEGISLATION

It is out of the scope of this manual to provide a full, up to date list of member state legislation. At the time of publication of this manual many member states are in the process of revising their legislation to incorporate EC directives.

The current situation can be obtained by contacting the following:

> Directorate-General V
> Employment, Industrial Relations and Social Affairs
> Rue de la Loi 2000
> B-1049 Brussels
> Belgium

Furthermore, a list of organisations responsible for SHE in EC member states is given in *Handbook of Labour Inspection (Health and Safety) in the European Community*, available from the Directorate General, Luxembourg.

PRIMARY UK LEGISLATION

Construction (Design & Management) Regulations 1994
Environment Protection Act 1990
Health and Safety at Work etc Act 1974
Control of Pollution Act 1974
Fire Precautions 1971
Pipelines Act 1962
Factories Act 1961

REGULATIONS

Control of Substances Hazardous to Health Regulations 1994
Control of Asbestos at Work (Amendment) Regulations 1992
Pressure Systems and Transportable Gas Containers Regulations 1992
Health and Safety (Display Screen Equipment) Regulations 1992
Manual Handling Operations Regulations 1992
Personal Protective Equipment at Work Regulations 1992
Provision and Use of Work Equipment Regulations 1992
Workplace (Health Safety and Welfare) Regulations 1992
Management of Health and Safety at Work Regulations 1992
The Control of Noise at Work Regulations 1989
The Electricity at Work Regulations 1989
Construction (Head Protection) Regulations 1989
The Reporting of Injuries, Diseases and Dangerous Occurrences Regulations
 (RIDDOR) 1985
Health and Safety (First Aid) Regulations 1981
The Control of Lead at Work Regulations 1980
Safety Signs Regulations 1980
Woodworking Machines Regulations 1974
Abrasive Wheels Regulations 1970
Construction (General Provisions) Regulations 1961
Construction (Health & Welfare) Regulations 1966
Construction (Working Places) Regulations 1966
Construction (Lifting Operations) Regulations 1961

Note:
The above list is not exhaustive but includes the main safety, health and environment
legislation applicable to construction activities in the UK. Other legislation will apply to
other activities, such as mines and quarries and work offshore etc.

CIRCUMSTANCES TO BE NOTIFIED TO THE HEALTH AND SAFETY EXECUTIVE IN UK

Similar requirements exist in other member states

		<u>FORM NO</u>
Accidents at Work *	Reporting of fatal or specified injuries	F2508
Notification of a Project	Project lasting longer than 30 days or 500 person days	F10 (Rev 03/95)
Notification of a Project	All demolition work	F10 (Rev 03/95)
Case of Disease *	Report of	F2508A
Dangerous Occurrences *	Reporting of	F2508

* See schedules included in the Reporting of Injuries, Diseases and Dangerous Occurrences Regulations 1985 (RIDDOR) Statutory Instrument SI 1985/2023

BIBLIOGRAPHY AND VIDEOS (UK)

BIBLIOGRAPHY

HEALTH AND SAFETY EXECUTIVE AND HEALTH AND SAFETY COMMISSION PUBLICATIONS

Refer to
- HSE PUBLIC ENQUIRY POINT, HSE Information Centre, Broad Lane, Sheffield S3 7HQ

- HSE BOOKS, PO Box 1999, Sudbury, Suffolk CO10 6FS

OTHER PUBLICATIONS

ARSCOTT, P.   **An employers guide to health and safety management.** Kogan Page for the Engineering Employers' Federation, 1976.

BIELLBY, S C. **Site Safety.** CIRIA, London, 1992.

BIRD, F.E. Jr.   **International safety rating system: general industry audit manual.** Institute Publishing, 1978.

BRITISH CONCRETE PUMPING ASSOCIATION   **BCPA manual and safety code of practice for concrete pumping.** BCPA, 1990.

BRITISH ELECTRICITY INTERNATIONAL.   **Modern power station practice - commissioning volume H.**   Pergamon Press, 1992.

BUILDING EMPLOYERS CONFEDERATION and BUILDING ADVISORY SERVICE.   **Construction safety.**   Building Employers Confederation and the Building Advisory Service. (periodically updated).

BUILDING EMPLOYERS CONFEDERATION and BUILDING ADVISORY SERVICE. **Site safety supervisors compendium.** Building Advisory Service. (periodically updated).

CHANNEL TUNNEL SAFETY AUTHORITY.   **Annual report 1989-90.** Channel Tunnel Safety Authority.

CHEMICAL INDUSTRIES ASSOCIATION. **A guide to hazard and operability studies.** Chemical Industries Association, 1977.

CONCRETE SOCIETY   **Formwork - a guide to good practice.** Concrete Society, 1986.

CONSTRUCTION INDUSTRY RESEARCH AND INFORMATION ASSOCIATION **A guide to reducing the exposure of construction workers to noise. Report no 120** CIRIA, 1990.

CONSTRUCTION INDUSTRY RESEARCH AND INFORMATION ASSOCIATION **A guide to the safe use of chemicals in construction.** SP16. CIRIA, 1981.

CONSTRUCTION INDUSTRY RESEARCH AND INFORMATION ASSOCIATION **Site safety handbook for young professionals.** CIRIA, expected 1992.

CONSTRUCTION INDUSTRY TRAINING BOARD. **Construction site safety course safety notes** (8 modules). Construction Industry Training Board, 1990.

CRONER'S **Croner's health and safety at work.** Croner, 1991.

CRONER'S **Croner's substances hazardous to health.** Croner, 1991.

KING, R.W. and HUDSON, R. **Construction hazard and safety handbook.** Butterworth, 1985.

LANEY, J. C. **Site safety.** Books on demand, 1982.

LAWLEY, H.G. Loss prevention; operability studies and hazard analysis. **Chemical Engineering Progress,** 1974, **70** (4), 45-56.

LEVITT, R E, SAMELSON, N M. **Contruction Safety Management (Second Edition).** John Wiley & Sons, Chichester, 1993.

NATIONAL ASSOCIATION OF SCAFFOLDING CONTRACTORS. **Scaffolders and users guide to safe access scaffolding.** NASC, 1987.

NATIONAL JOINT COUNCIL FOR THE BUILDING INDUSTRY. **Site safe and you.** NJCBI, 1986.

NATIONAL JOINT COUNCIL FOR THE BUILDING INDUSTRY. **Site safe and your health.** NJCBI, 1989.

OIL AND CHEMICAL PLANT CONSTRUCTORS ASSOCIATION. **Safety manual for mechanical plant construction.** Building Advisory Service, 1991.

REDGRAVE, A. **Health and safety.** Butterworth, 1990.

STRANKS, J.W. **Manager's guide to health and safety at work.** Kogan Page, 1990.

VIDEOS

Acts and omissions. RoSPA Film Library. 35 minutes.

Alive or dead (electrical safety). Health and Safety Executive. 21 minutes.

A Safer Bet - An Introduction to the Principles of the CDM Regulations 1994. Construction Industry Council. 35 minutes.

Be alive to safety - piling operations (general, piling). Construction Industry Training Board. 20 minutes.

Beginner's luck. Introducing the lessons of site safety to new employees (general, civil). Longman Training. 20 minutes.

Blind man's buff. Active practice in spotting potential disasters before they happen. (hazard spotting, general). Longman Training. 19 minutes.

Blind man's buff. Active practice in spotting potential disasters before they happen. Summary film (hazard spotting, general). Longman Training. 6 minutes.

Building sites bite. CFL Vision. 26 minutes.

Collapse - what to do (first aid for heart attack). Health and Safety Specifier. 15 minutes.

Contract (The). Working with outside contractors brings its own special demands (contract management, general). Longman Training. 22 minutes.

COSHH in practice. A guide to the Control of Substances Hazardous to Health Regulations (substances hazardous to health). Longman Training. 21 minutes.

COSHH in practice. A guide to the Control of Substances Hazardous to Health Regulations. Legislation film (substances hazardous to health). Longman Training. 6 minutes.

COSHH - making a start. Costains. 17 minutes.

COSHH - on site. Costains. 13 minutes.

Cost of chaos. Preventing accidents by careful site maintenance. Longman Millbank. 11 minutes.

Danger zone hands (hands). Video Arts Distribution Ltd. 20 minutes.

Dummy run (general). National Engineering Contractors Employers Association. 18 minutes.

Hangman. Falls are the biggest risk on construction sites (falls, people). Longman Training. 15 minutes.

Hearing conservation. A management overview (hearing protection, management). Technical Video Library. 12 minutes.

I can't see. Sight is a vital sense; eye protection makes for common sense. Longman Training. 22 minutes.

I'm sorry what's that you said? (hearing protection, general). Technical Video Library. 15 minutes.

In your own interest. CCD Product Design. 18 minutes.

Is there anything I've forgotten? Permit to work systems for confined spaces. Longman Training. 21 minutes.

Live safely with steel (steelwork erection safety, falls). Visual Link Production Centre. 12 minutes.

Mobile towers. Construction Industry Training Board. 15 minutes.

No questions asked. Site safety on the construction site is everyone's concern (excavations, trench collapse). Longman Training. 17 minutes.

Not Just an Accident....Training for Young Professionals. CIRIA. 31 minutes.

Off your trolley (roofwork). WC Youngman. 10 minutes.

Office safety. John Burder Films. 14 minutes.

Overhead power cables. Construction Industry Training Board. 14 minutes.

Plan your slinging (slinging). Health and Safety Executive. 16 minutes.

Safe under pressure (gas bottles, weld/cutting gear). BOC Ltd. 18 minutes.

Safety at work. John Burder Films. 15 minutes.

Safety first, second and third. Electrical Contractors Association. 15 minutes.

Safety on site (general). QI Training Ltd. 25 minutes.

A site safer. Spreading the message of safety throughout a busy building site (general, CITB). Longman Training. 28 minutes.

So you're in charge. CHSG. 21 minutes.

Trenching. A grave affair. Videotel International. 15 minutes.

Trenching good practice. Construction Industry Research and Information Association. 11 minutes.

Understanding weld fume (weld fume, COSHH). ICI, Welding Institute, Health and Safety Executive. 20 minutes.

Unreasonably dead. Why Electricity at Work Regulations are there to help and protect (electrical safety). Longman Training. 25 minutes.

Unreasonably dead. Why Electricity at Work Regulations are there to help and protect. Legislation film. (electrical safety). Longman Training. 6 minutes.

Watch that space (construction) (confined spaces). CFL Vision. 16 minutes.

Watch that space (factories) (confined spaces). CFL Vision. 16 minutes.

Watch that space (shipbuilding) (confined spaces). CFL Vision. 15 minutes.

Where's Danny? High level, high-risk dangers - safety in the painting industry. (falls). Longman Training. 15 minutes.

VIDEO PRODUCERS

BOC Ltd The Priestley Centre 10 Priestley Road The Surrey Research Park Guildford Surrey GU2 5XY United Kingdom

CCD Product Design Ltd 76 Church Street Weybridge Surrey KT13 8DL United Kingdom

CFL Vision PO Box 35 Wetherby West Yorkshire LS23 7EX United Kingdom

CHSG John Ryder Centre St Ann's Road Chertsey Surrey KT16 9DD United Kingdom

Construction Industry Training Board Bircham Newton Kings Lynn Norfolk PE31 6RH United Kingdom

Costains Costain House West Street Woking Surrey GU21 1EU United Kingdom

Electrical Contractors Association 34 Palace Court London W2 United Kingdom

Health and Safety Executive Broad Lane Sheffield S3 7HQ United Kingdom

Health and Safety Specifier 32 Portland Street Cheltenham Gloucestershire GL52 2PB United Kingdom

John Burder Films 7 Saltcoats Road London W4 1AR United Kingdom

Longman Millbank/Longman Training Longman House Burnt Hill Harlow Essex CM20 2JE United Kingdom

National Engineering Contractors Employers Association Broadway House Tothill Street London SW1H 9NQ United Kingdom

QI Training Ltd 2 The Green Lydiard Millicent Swindon Wiltshire SN5 9LP United Kingdom

RoSPA Film Library Cannon House Priory Queensway Birmingham 4 United Kingdom

Technical Video Library Hadlow House 9 The High Street Green Street Green Farnborough Kent United Kingdom

Video Arts Distribution Ltd Dumbarton House 68 Oxford Street London W1N 9LA United Kingdom

Videotel International Ramillies House 1 Ramillies Street London W1V 1DF United Kingdom

Visual Link Production Centre Kingstown Broadway Carlisle Cumbria CA3 0HA United Kingdom

WC Youngman 374a Wandsworth Road London SW8 4TH United Kingdom